OF THE

Afterlife

■

The Conversation
Continues

Br. Gary Joseph, s.F.m.

Mercy Books
Servants of the Father of Mercy, Inc.

Los Angeles

PROOF OF THE AFTERLIFE
The Conversation Continues _____

Being published by arrangement with the author.

To order additional copies, or for more information, email:
Info@ServantsoftheFather.org.

Or write:

PROOF OF THE AFTERLIFE
Servants of the Father of Mercy
P. O. Box 42001
Los Angeles, CA 90042

Get in touch with the author to schedule a group presentation or
speaking engagement by sending an email request to
Contact@ServantsoftheFather.org.

ISBN: 978-0-615-41009-8

Dedication

Proof of the Afterlife – The Conversation Continues is enthusiastically and gratefully dedicated to Fr. F., an insightful Spiritual Director and friend.

MERCY BOOKS

Published by Servants of the Father of Mercy, Inc.

P. O. Box 42001, Los Angeles, CA 90042

First *Mercy Books* edition published November 2010
by special arrangement with the author

Library of Congress Cataloging-in-Publication Data
Joseph, Gary Br.
Proof of the Afterlife – *The Conversation Continues*
1. Spiritual life – Catholic Church 2. Christianity

ISBN 978-0-615-41009-8

Note of Thanks

On July 30, 2010, this book's manuscript was sent to the archbishop of the Archdiocese of Los Angeles, Cardinal Roger Mahony for theological review three months in advance of its publication. I offer many thanks to Cardinal Mahony, his priest assistants and theological team for having received the manuscript and for perusing its content.

Also, I send many prayers and blessings to Fr. F., my spiritual director for the time he took to read, and offer feedback in the nascent stages of the book's creation.

Last but not least, *Proof of the Afterlife – The Conversation Continues,* was lovingly evaluated and edited by Pam, Angela and Anita and her mom Mildred. God bless each of you for all your time, insights, passion and effort.

TABLE OF CONTENTS

PROLOGUE

The Bilheimer Cabin

As I write *Proof of the Afterlife – The Conversation Continues,* I'm holed up for many days in a mountain cabin that a friend so generously provided. It's in the high desert of the San Gabriel Mountains, and although no one is here, one can't help but to hear the conversation that is going on all around.

Right now it is springtime. Nature seems to have a unique dialogue with itself and with the visitors that come here this time of year, very different from summer, fall and winter I would imagine. For instance, there are a plethora of birds and their new born little ones that congregate around the cabin, mostly in the morning at sunrise. Some sing, some chirp, squawk, squeal and yet others even seem to talk. I thought only humans did that! The chipmunks, baby rabbits, jack rabbits and the ground squirrels all play in the moment and somehow everyone seems to get along, surprisingly, really well.

Up here, around five thousand feet above the Pacific Ocean, the wind seems to howl with mysterious utterances too, especially in the springtime. You can never see the wind – from where it comes or where it goes, but it's always a surprise when a forceful gust coaxes the car off a mountain road, like a dry leaf aimlessly flopping about in the desert below. It's times like this that the wind seems to tell everyone that it's in charge in this neck of the woods. When I first arrived, the winds were calm and balmy. Last night they had a mind of their own and they were frigid – powerfully gusting particles of desert sand and pinecones all the way to Kansas! That particular exchange told me to stay inside, build a fire and snuggle up because it's going to be a long boisterous night. It was.

Living in the desert has taught me to be obedient to the sun when it talks – in these parts, the sun rules. In the springtime, that ninety-three-million-mile-away fireball wakes up pretty darn early. At about 5:30am, the first rays of soft blue and orange light ever so gently begin to bathe the front kitchen window, which incidentally has no curtain on it. It's a cabin with a view, so while doing the dishes dialoguing with the twinkling valley lights at sunset, or grey stormy clouds below in the morning, one needs to be ready and waiting with no hindrances, like a drape obstructing the chatter. But let's get back to the 5:30am first soft rays of dawn's early light. By 6:00am, the blaring luminous streams of sunbeams burst into the cabin vociferously crying out, *"Wake up; it's time to get up!"* There's no escaping that conversation, no matter how tired you are or how hard you try. It's just time to obey, crawl out of bed and make a nice freshly brewed cup of hot coffee.

The mountains and hills all around have a wonderful babble, too. These are majestic old mounts that in the parching hundred-degree desert heat of summer, might say, *"Go away, there's nothing to look at right now,"* but not so in the spring. At the moment, lush green wilderness cactus blossom everywhere with delicate white and pink blooms. The neighboring shrubs and ground cover sprout royal purple, white and deep yellow flora. All of it seems to create a symphony of voices that croon, *"Look at us. Look at the mountains and hills. We've gotten ready for your visit. Resurrection has come. Rejoice!"*

What's most remarkable is how much of the discussion here goes on in silence. Yes, the silence speaks volumes. Far from the distractions of urban life like idle chatter, whining, complaining, going to the store for this-or-that, meetings and phone calls – life here is so very silent, so purged of fast food and other modern addictions that its emptiness tells the conversation within to speak out. That's frightening sometimes. Possibly it's easier in the city where one does not have to wrestle with the silence. But here you do. It's all good though. In the end, I'm thankful I stuck out my many days in solitude on this mountain. The hush gave birth to the voice of this book, *Proof of the Afterlife – The Conversation Continues*. How remarkable and extraordinary to enter into the silence to write a book about dialogue. Only God could orchestrate that anomaly!

Lastly, the cabin itself is a conversation. How so you may ask? Well, the Bilheimer family has been coming to this mountain retreat for more than fifty years, long before there were any civil roads to get here. Back then, the trip from the coast took hours and provided for a lot of the folks time to just chat in the car on the way up. On the walls, there are pictures of grandpa Bilheimer posing with '40s politicians – that tells a story too. Other old photographs of the children, grandchildren and great-grandchildren are hung up on what looks like aged California redwood paneling. According to the clothing of the time, some of the photos look as though they were taken straight from a 60s television shoot of *"Father's Know Best"* or *"Leave it to Beaver."* Also, not far from the charred, stone fireplace, are inviting pictures of snowy winter days, an Indian-themed Thanksgiving fiesta and lots of plain ol' black and white family shots. All of which seem to say that here are relatives who know how to pursue and enjoy engaging conversations with each other. Hopefully, now that everyone has read this prologue, we'll all go out and be stirred to do more of the same. Thank you DJ, Susan and family for the cabin, the inspiration and the conversation. Thank you to Pam and Joel for making the connection.

CHAPTER ONE

Introduction to the Conversation

In the early hours of the morning of September 27th, I had awoken at 1:00am feeling energetic and unable to sleep. After a few minutes, I got up and stood in the living room with some pillows, a blanket and the television's remote control in hand, somewhat expecting that a round or two of late-night shows might help me to fall back asleep. As I glanced at the DVD player, it was now 1:15am. What happens next is recorded as the first entry in a journal that would eventually chronicle five years of repeated encounters with the Other Side. Here is what I wrote that startling night at two o'clock in the morning.

Tuesday, September 27, 2005 – It is 2:00am in the morning and I will try to put into words the gift of "seeing" and experiencing the presence of God, the Father Almighty and his son, the Lord Jesus Christ. At 1:00am this morning, I awoke after just a couple of hours of sleep and was going to watch television with a pillow and blanket on the living room floor. Instead, in the darkness, while the television clock read 1:15am, I decided to try and fall asleep on the floor and get some additional rest. Just as I began to turn over to fall asleep, I was overcome by an enormous Presence that came into the room and filled the atmosphere all around me. Initially, I did not know Who or What this Presence was, but I was terrified.

Physically weakened, by the shock of an overwhelming supernatural Power densely saturating the room, I grasped the edge of the dining room table in hopes to give my legs strength to run and hide. I attempted to run away three times. However, I was completely overcome and could not stand on my own ability. I was only able to make it to my knees, but then I had to surrender to this Almighty Power and fell to the floor yielding to its Presence and control. At this point, I was fearful, yet I felt strangely safe giving in to this Power. My heart raced and beat out of my chest. My body felt as though it would burst from His Presence. My hands and feet felt as though they would explode.

After I collapsed on the floor, I had a sense that I had died. My heart stopped, it became extremely quiet and all the energy – an intense electrical tingling sensation exited out of my hands and feet. Next, in the solitude, I hovered over my body for a brief moment and saw myself, my body collapsed on the floor. Immediately I left the living room and I was facing the front of a gray screen. I was powerfully aware that I was now in the presence of God the Father Almighty. The gray screen was shielding me from His pure white rays of radiant and piercing glory. Some pieces of brilliant light escaped and passed through small holes in the screen, but God chose to shield me from His complete presence. Spontaneously, I said over and over to Him, *"Glory to God in the highest and peace to His people on earth."* He identified Himself as the God of the Bible, the God of Abraham, Isaac and Jacob. He did not speak the way we do; his communication seemed absorbed, like a crashing tsunami wave soaking into a dry sandy beach.

Next, I asked if I could see Him. He responded to me with a simple but emphatic, *"No!"* He said, *"No, you cannot see me or you will be dead."* He revealed to me that He cannot expose me to His complete glory, that I could not survive such an experience. He made known to me many lifetimes of Biblical and theological studies in what seemed like seconds. He spoke of His character, He is my Father and He created me. He revealed His Fatherhood qualities are composed of duty, righteousness, honor, high expectations, labor, love, steadfastness and judgment. He communicated not in linear thoughts, but by instant absorption, transmitting millions of messages that flooded my soul in a brief moment.

Then I was taken from His presence and began to drift aimlessly in total blackness, as if I was in some remote part of outer space. At first, I was terrified of the dark and the void. Yet, the thought occurred to me that I had just been with God the Father, there is nothing to fear. I began to have faith. At the moment of having faith, my feet landed on solid ground and I felt more secure in the darkness. As I looked around, I was transfixed on a small speck of light way out in the black universe. I watched as it came closer to the planet. It appeared to be my only hope in the vast darkness. The light, so it turns out, was actually a great, magnificent, luminous white cross radiating powerful beams, piercing the blackness and slicing through the void in an indescribable way – unlike any illumination we have here on earth. It powerfully cut through the blackness of the night. Instantly, I realized that this light is Christ, as it grew in radiance above me. I recognized Jesus in his *"sign of the cross."* Upon realizing that it was Jesus, He immediately came from the cross, flooded me with love, mercy and hugs that exceed millions of times more than any earthly love and hugs a child could ever receive from a mother or father. As he caressed me with His love and presence, I said to him over and over, *"A day in your presence, Lord, is better than thousands elsewhere."* I wanted to stay right there in His arms forever.

However, in those very moments while I was being embraced by Christ, I was sent back to my body. I awoke on the living room floor and saw that the clock in front of me now said 1:45am. I had been like a dead man, immersed in this encounter for exactly thirty minutes. My heart had restarted again and it was pounding out of my chest. With every beat, the chest lifted high from my body and I felt as though my heart and my chest would explode. It seemed as though my body could not sustain the soul's direct encounter with God.

Not at any time did I ever feel as though this was a medical emergency and never did I think about calling for help. To the contrary, I recalled over and over in my mind the events that had just occurred. I had just "seen" God! I was completely overcome, dazed and confused as to what it all meant. I lay there some minutes, hoping to gain strength and the ability to walk again after absorbing the complete impact and shock of the event. At 2:00am I stood up, weak and trembling and wrote in my computer this account of what had just happened.

As a footnote to this momentous encounter, that same day, weak and still overcome by a collision with God's presence, I somehow mustered up the ability to go to work as usual and then attended the daily 5:30pm Mass that I had begun going to the past couple of months. After receiving Communion, I spoke with Fr. Ed in the church parking lot about the extraordinary event that had just taken place. Shaken, overwhelmed and feeling internally corrupt to the core because I had been exposed to the purity of God, I went to Confession for the first time in decades. I remarked to Fr. Ed that no human should be allowed to be in the presence of God, especially me! I was both doomed and cleansed by the illuminating presence of God granting me full knowledge of my worthlessness. I was unworthy to have been there and repeatedly asked myself, *"Why me?"* After what happened today, I feel like I can relate in a very small way and also eerily echo the words of Isaiah the prophet, who after having been caught up into heaven and seeing the presence of God, he wrote: *"Woe is me! For I am lost; for I am a man of unclean lips; and I dwell in the midst of a people of unclean lips; for my eyes have seen the King, the Lord of hosts."* (Isaiah 6:5)

Reading this incredible account, some might feel that one extraordinary encounter would be enough of a conversation with God to convince anyone to believe in him and reform their ways. However, this book is not about one meeting with Eternity. After the events of September 27th, a cascade of supernatural meetings began to take place, surprising me, my spiritual director, mother, family and friends at every turn. I will share their details throughout the book, just as recorded when they happened.

In hindsight, now I realize that God was having a conversation with me all my life. I suspect not only me, but he is having it with every person he has ever created. For this reason, it became apparent to me to share with others my on-going dialogue with the other side. Those willing to read the entire book, may it awaken within each, the ability to hear the voice of God speaking in our lives today.

So what is this conversation all about? Our English word *"conversation"*, prior to its use in Middle English and French, came to us in ancient times. Its root is from the Latin word *'conversari'* which means *"to associate with."* Nowadays, we primarily think of the word *"conversation"* to mean *"a discussion or an exchange of thoughts and ideas."* It is refreshing to add the Latin root *'conversari'* to the mix. It is here, in this added dimension that this book uses the word *"conversation."* Meaning, it is not simply a discussion or an exchange of ideas between family, friends or colleagues. At its very core, *"conversation"* is first and foremost an intimate and life-giving *'association'* with others. In that light, let us begin.

The whole world is a conversation isn't it? When we are newborn babies, we struggle to enter into that conversation. After months of incoherent sounds, one day and completely unexpectedly, babies suddenly explode with first words like, *Da Da* or a hearty, *Ma Ma*! Next, we spend most of our childhood going to school where we learn the alphabet and then on to history, science, languages and math, so we can grow up and competently participate in the entire conversation around us.

Ever plan a trip to a foreign country? The first thing to do is get a crash course in their language. It's very important to engage in the conversation once you arrive there isn't it? Conversing with the locals is no doubt rooted in the desire to associate with others around us – the people in airports, cafes, bars, restaurants, shops and museums. Dialoguing at every turn is at the very core of what we will do each and every minute while visiting that country.

Our desire to have conversation and association with others is so strong, that most people would like to believe that the conversation we are having now with our loved ones, somehow even continues after their death. This desire is so innate in the human experience, that long before Christianity reached ancient cultures in the Americas, the Mayans, the Aztecs and other Indian tribes had firmly established beliefs in the afterlife. Our celebration of Halloween, in fact, has gained popularity around the world beyond the U.S. in recent years.

The fall celebration provides many a chance to think about and even have fun with the notion of souls being fully alive in the hereafter. Acknowledging life after death and having contact with these souls, is at the core of most cultures and peoples' experience.

Although some may struggle with the idea of life after death, still others firmly believe that it is also possible to even converse with God himself. According to very ancient records of the Bible, Abraham spoke with God and Moses did too. Many saints and modern mystics have been said to have conversed with God as well. As recent as the mid-1900s, right prior to World War II, a small unassuming nun in the country of Poland, by the name of Faustina Kowalska, experienced frequent and direct conversations with God. Her astonishing mystical encounters are meticulously detailed in a six-hundred page journal titled, *Diary of Maria Faustina Kowalska*, available at most bookstores.

Thus, taking all things into consideration throughout the ages, it seems as though the conversation in our lives is actually a lot bigger than possibly could be imagined – spanning both heaven and earth. The cosmic dialogue that is going on around us is much grander than all our cell phone calls, texting and emails combined! However, the caveat is that one can't even hear or participate, if belief in God is rejected. God's conversation is reserved only for people of Faith, those who are humbly searching for truth and who hunger and thirst for righteousness.

Not only has God been having a conversation and association with the world since its inception, but we too have been experiencing the same with each other. Our families, friends, nations and even foes have also been striving to be in conversation with each other since the beginning of civilization. Life itself – living here on this earth, is one big exchange with each other and with God.

Most people attend religious services at one time or another because of our inborn desire to speak with God and in hope that he speaks back to us. But also with our family and friends, our lives are centered on this sort of grand chatter going on all around us. For instance, we take meals together, we sit and have coffee together, we go out for a drink, we go for a walk together and what do we do? We chat, and we chat, and we chat! That is why when a friend or loved one dies, our immediate reaction is to miss calling them, to miss visiting them, going out together and ultimately, we miss conversing with them. And where do we eventually end up when we have anxieties about these matters? We head back to church and in our "cloud of unknowing" we try to initiate a dialogue with God.

Of course, most know, on some interior level, that the Bible – the Holy Scriptures are a key chunk of God's conversation with all of us here on earth. The Bible is the number one bestselling book of all time. The Book has sold in the billions of copies since the invention of the printing press. No other book has ever or will ever come close to this literary sales record. It is unbeatable, and for good reason. In it, God himself has a discussion with us about our individual and collective human condition. The Scriptures are authoritative and we can count on them to frame what God has to say to us about being in association with him, going to heaven and enjoying eternal life.

Through this collection of ancient manuscripts, written primarily in Hebrew and Greek, and assembled over thousands of years of history (no other book in the records of the world has ever been compiled in this way), God converses with us individually and corporately. He shows us that illness, suffering and death are not what he had planned for us. We discover that humans, at one point in ancient time, cut ties with God and quit effectively conversing with him and with each other. When we decided to go it alone, our association with each other also suffered gravely. Shortly after the first sin, the "Big Screw Up" in the Garden of Eden, as the story goes, Cain kills Abel and the first of millions of murders takes place in human history. Now, today in hindsight, we all know what the Garden's first sin of human pride, arrogance and declaration of independence from God has gotten us – wars, violence, crime, murder, injustice, inequity and the like.

But God is merciful and has steadfastly conversed with us over the ages, with the goal to put each one of us, all of humankind back on track – to reorder our lives, to reorder our passions so that we can enter into peace and eternal life. It has been his goal to create cosmos out of chaos, which God is infinitely good at according to the "Big Bang Theory." His aim has been to take our "disconnect" and re-establish the connection, no matter what the personal cost is to him or us.

However, God's conversation with us does not end at the close of the last book of the Bible. In every age, he also speaks to each one of us through nature as well as through our hearts, minds and souls – right within the context of our daily lives. He is no doubt having a dialogue with each of his children at this very moment. But some are so busy or don't even care, that they are not listening. They become endlessly wrapped up in worldly pursuits that unequivocally silence the voice of God. As a result, many believe that God does not exist or doubt that he exists because they are deaf to his conversation.

Each of us here, on the earth today, is just as special to him as the Biblical writers he once directly inspired – Isaiah, Esther, Jeremiah, Ruth, Peter, James or John. His conversation continues with each of us just as it did in the days of old. It is a common mistake to think that God's "words" and "mighty deeds" are told only in Scripture. Every person's heart and life is etched with God's "words." We are imprinted with his creative expression of art, goodness, compassion and love that interiorly speak to each one of us loud and clear in our daily lives. God talks first and foremost in our hearts, minds and conscience. But he also speaks through friends, events in our lives, situations we find ourselves in, family, nature and the spiritual writings of the saints.

However, what is most remarkable, God also piques our interest in his words of life through "supernatural" means. Many call it "supernatural", but I like to think of it as "natural." Through his "natural" ways, God speaks to us in dreams, our personal prayer times, church services and even provides some with visions, bi-locations (Padre Pio) and various types of auditory and interior locutions (cf. Teresa of Avila and John of the Cross). The point of the matter is that God cares and he *is* speaking – even today, this very minute! Some may have not taken the time or the effort to stay in touch, so they think he doesn't care or worse yet, *"God is dead!"*

Having a book like this, to validate that the conversation is on and hotly engaging, is very encouraging for many. That is why I am writing the manuscript. As I stated in the Prologue, I have taken some weeks off work to be holed up in this mountain cabin to do one thing, to carve hope out of human hearts – some made of flesh and yet others of stone. To give encouragement to the many that struggle to know about the marvelous winds of God's Spirit aggressively at work, dusting off our lives and blowing new life into our hearts today.

If you are like me, possibly you have never known or met someone that has had visions, locutions and conversations with God or with souls from the other side. Frankly, I am the first person I have ever known or met in this regard. Now, I am learning of many others as I share my story. Since completing the study of undergraduate and graduate-level theology in 1978, I've been experiencing "natural" phenomena from the other side from time-to-time. However, since my near-death-experience (NDE) in 2005, and then recent theological studies at St. John's

Seminary, the encounters have increased significantly and I have been gifted with sometimes two – three events a week. I imagine many of these gifts are not for me, but to share for the building up of Faith in others like you. Many miraculous interventions recorded in my journal I will share in the following chapters of this book in order that you may have hope in God – hope for your life, as well as hope for your family and friends' lives; that you may also have peace and have it abundantly.

At this point, there may be more questions raised than answers. Of course, it is only the introduction, so give time for the following pages to make known my story and I will also try to address your concerns. So what are the many questions one may have and that people might be asking about the possibility of having authentic conversations with God and the souls on the other side? Will the obvious questions be covered in this book?

Yes, *Proof of the Afterlife – The Conversation Continues,* will shed light on the following: How do we hear from God? How do we enter into a conversation with him? Just as importantly, how do we enter into life-giving conversations with each other in the midst of being preoccupied with our work, commuting, household responsibilities and the like? Does the conversation with a loved one end at their death? Does the conversation end with God upon our own death? What happens to us when we die? How do we enter into conversation with family and friends who have crossed over to the other side? Can they hear us? Can we hear them? What is the ultimate purpose of this cosmic dialogue when we actually tune into it?

What happens at a person's funeral – are they there – can they see and hear us? Does God continue conversing with souls who have departed? Do they receive more chances to "get it right"? Can we help them? Can they help us? Is this a book just about the dead? How will the evidence in this book help the living? Will it help me to live a better life? What are the lessons to be learned here?

Wow, that's a lot of questions! But you probably have dozens more. After all, we are talking about the very nature of eternity here – that's an endless bundle of information. However, I suspect that by the time you finish reading *Proof of the Afterlife – The Conversation Continues,* you will have a sense that many of your questions will have been addressed and possibly even resolved. But how will you know that? That's a good question too. Don't take my word for it. The proof is in the peace! There will be a growing peace in your heart and mind as you read. There will arise, deep within, a sense that you are tapping into the very nature, the very truth of who *God Is.* (He tells Moses, [my name is], *"I am."*) The proof is in the peace that will saturate your soul, like fresh bread dunked in a wonderful coffee or tea, but millions of times more satisfying!

Okay, let's be real. There may be even more proof for some readers. What do I mean by that? Well, I suspect that what God has done for me, by opening up the flood gates of conversation on all sides, he wants to do the same for the many who are reading this book; mainly because of your sincere desire to seek after him. God wants to have ongoing dialogue with you as well as with your loved ones, no doubt. There may be a need for souls on the other side to "speak" with you, especially if there is the unfinished business of love and forgiveness to be worked out. All it takes on your part is a humble heart, daily prayer, charity and an open mind to accept all that the limitless Lord God has to offer. It is more about coming to God in poverty, acknowledging our sinfulness and emptiness than it is about knowing, wanting to know, pride or wealth.

If you sincerely wish to have merciful and compassionate relationships with your family and friends, whether dead or alive, God wants to open up the dialogue for you here on earth and with the other side. If you have a sincere desire to forgive others, to be patient, kind and compassionate as God has done for you, God wants to hook you up to where all the chatter is. However, if you are stuck in unforgiveness, hate, anger, unbelief and other negative emotions – it is important to know that the gifts of heaven are reserved only for those who have faith, forgive and pray blessings for one's enemies. Now would be a good time to begin to pray for those who have hurt you and whom you have hurt, and make a decision to become merciful toward them – whether they are dead or alive. Just as God is being merciful toward us in our failures, sins and shortcomings – so must we be that way with others. The more heroically merciful that you are, the more likely it is that God will be gracious toward you and open the flood gates of heavenly conversation with him and with others.

For those who have a Catholic heritage or would like to have one, the Sacraments of the Church can help big time to facilitate this dialogue with God and with each other. To this point, here is an entry from my journal just a few weeks after my near-death-experience:

Friday, October 14, 2005 – Attending daily Mass and Communion has become for me the sign and symbol and the reality that all through my life, Jesus Christ has longed to have an on-going Communion, a constant dialogue with me. Minute-by-minute he wishes to talk with me and to walk with me. Second-by-second He wishes to reveal his presence to me. Going to daily Mass and Communion brings me into an eternal perpetual conversation with Christ, very God himself. Daily Communion fills me with a constant moment-by-moment presence of God in my life, as initially revealed in the encounter of September 27, 2005, when right prior to it, for two months I had begun to go to daily Mass and Communion.

Going forward, as the story unravels; you will discover that this book's chapters are named after my family associations, all leading to the point that the conversation does indeed continue with loved ones, dead or alive. Ranging from a chapter starting with myself, to chapters about how the conversation has played out with loved ones such as my brother, father, mother, cousin as well as other family and friends.

CHAPTER TWO

Me

I planned, for a while now, to open up this chapter with a particular clip from my journal, because its reflection gives hope to all those who see themselves as weak, lost, broken and a sinner. I am a first-hand witness to the fact that a loser is exactly the kind of person that God loves in a special way and wants to talk to. Yes, I am a contemporary "eyewitness" to God, but that is only because I am a sinner like everyone else on the planet. It would be inaccurate for anyone to think that I am anything "special" because of the enormous gift I have received by directly encountering God. My eyewitness account should not make anyone feel envious or slighted, but to the contrary, it should make us all feel strengthened and filled with hope that God goes after the "ordinary" as well as those who are empty and broken. Almost two years after my near-death-experience, I wrote the following in my journal in this regard:

―――――――――――

Wednesday, July 18, 2007 – In a vision this morning, I was standing in a large hall filled with many people. I got up and addressed the crowd and said to them, "*It is significant for you that a sinner like me has encountered the Lord. Although you were not there* [at my Paul-like, NDE] *you accept my testimony.*

It is a message of hope, that God likewise is revealing himself to you. He loves you and wants to have a relationship with you."

———————————

Now, here's a little bit of my story . . . In the summer of 2005, I was suddenly diagnosed with a tumor – a large growth about the size of a golf ball attached to the thyroid. In April, I had been examined for two days by one of the top hospitals in the country and it was their professional opinion that the on-again, off-again rapid heart arrhythmias and sensations of suffocation I had been experiencing for a few years were psychological and they recommended Prozac. I refused to take it. However, it was in June that a medical student accidentally picked out my x-rays for class work and discovered a golf-ball-size tumor growing interiorly in my throat, compressing on the airway. The doctor in charge called me apologetically and said to come in immediately; he suspected, given the size, it was going to test positive for cancer.

About that very same time, my cousin Kim (who was a childhood favorite and adult business partner too), living 3,000 miles away, was about to go on a scuba diving expedition. After a routine checkup on a Monday, on the following Friday, what she thought would be a regular day of receiving normal test results, turned out to be the doctor telling her that she had extensive lung cancer and was being given about 6-9 months to live.

Although I had been very "busy" for the past twenty-one years as a writer and business consultant and had made very little time for God, I knew that had to immediately change. In July of 2005, though working 9-5 at the time, I had made a decision to attend daily Mass and Communion for the special intention of my cousin Kim, her well-being and for myself and my own health woes. The Mass was at 5:30pm and that meant I had no ability to work overtime and be a workaholic like I had done for decades. Establishing a dialogue and a relationship with God was now a top priority.

Up until the middle of August, when inpatient surgery was scheduled, the medical professionals were thinking "cancer" because two different biopsies came back inconclusive. However, the day the surgery was performed, afterwards in O.R., the tumor was immediately tested by frozen section and it miraculously came back negative! After some weeks of daily prayer and Mass, a miracle had taken place. Likewise, my cousin Kim had begun aggressive cancer treatments at a hospital in Houston, Texas, and was commuting by air 2,000 miles a week. Through the advancements of modern medicine, and I believe various miracles from God, Kim out-lived her prognosis (by one-and-a-half years) and had a much fuller life than expected. One miracle that stands out in my mind was the day Kim, had succumb to undiagnosed fluid building up around her heart. "Coincidentally," she was walking into the hospital for a regularly scheduled check-up when she went into cardiac arrest. The professional and timely treatment she received, added many more quality months to her life. She died on May 30, 2007. Kim was 49 years old.

I recovered well after my surgery. Within 24 hours I was sent home from the hospital and within two weeks I was back to work and had begun attending daily Mass and Communion again. But in August, my thoughts were turning more contemplative than before and not as self-centered as I normally was in life. In my college years, I had dedicated myself to completing a Bachelor of Theology degree and a Masters in Biblical Studies and quite actively served God. Since that time, I had drifted away from my conversation with God – that is up until now.

In August of 2005, I had returned to reading the Scriptures once again. In the first moment that I had flipped open my old tattered Bible dating back to the '70s, I accidentally and quite randomly turned to this first sentence after twenty-one years away, *"This I have against you, you have lost your first love."* (Revelations 2:4) Whoa! There was no doubt in my mind that God was having a conversation with me and it was spanning the length and breadth of my lifetime.

In that August, I was also thinking a lot about my dad as I was resting, healing and getting stronger from the surgery. He had passed away in July of 2003. He was a harsh man in many ways and in today's terms he would be called "abusive." He was tough with almost everyone – his wife, children and co-workers – no one was exempt. Confusingly, at times he could also be very charming and cordial too. However, what bothered me the most in this relationship was his cavalier ability to behave belligerently and somehow justify it all in the name of religion. I guess that would be called a type of "hypocrisy." For decades, it was tough to forgive all that had happened to so many of us at his hands. But suddenly, I was coming to a more accurate realization about myself and frequently saying interiorly, *"Hey, you're a loser! You're a sinner too. Your sin is just different from his."* That insight helped me to muster up the mercy and compassion necessary to genuinely forgive him. It felt good when it all came together in my mind in those weeks right after surgery. It seemed as though the conversation was opening up, but I had no idea at this point how huge it was going to get.

A few weeks after the near-death-experience, I saw my family physician for a regular follow-up visit and he diagnosed the event as a heart attack caused by a rapid arrhythmia which was set off by a thyroid that was healing (from where the growth was removed). The thyroid had momentarily become hyperactive. He and his nursing staff gathered and listened intently as I shared the details of the NDE. The doctor, convinced that what had happened to me was real, said candidly, *"Dude, you've been somewhere where few people ever return from. I have had a few other patients over the years that have described very similar after death experiences."*

In the days and weeks that followed this enormous God-encounter, I began to journal. To this very day, almost five years later, I keep record of many reflections, illuminations, thoughts, visions and locutions. I will be sharing various entries from my journal in the chapters that follow.

There is no doubt that when God reveals himself in such an amazing manner, that the revelation is a complete gift. Everything is a gift – our salvation, sanctification, faith and even being connected to God himself. I realize that I bring nothing to the table. It is all grace, it is all a gift. I have done nothing to deserve anything. I am the very least to have received such an enormous prize!

In hindsight, I have begun to realize that not just these mountain top revelations of God are a gift, but also his pursuit of us over the total years of our life is a gift too. It is apparent to me now, that God comes after us in a way that he allows the gifts of suffering, afflictions and illness in order to bring us to himself. It is very similar to the athlete, who suffers greatly while in training, just to win an Olympic Games competition. While preparing, the coach allows his protégé to feel the pain, knowing the value of the great prize to be won. Thus, suffering truly is a gift. It can help us to become perfected into a peaceful state of quietude, by divesting one from the daily internal noise of self-seeking activities that crowd out God's voice.

Ultimately, how does suffering work its magic? It has the unique ability to temporarily suspend – arrest one's free will by creating a type of Purgatory here on earth. Thereby, the way is paved for the soul to become wonderfully tranquil; thus giving the person the phenomenal ability to be directly united in conversation with very God himself.

CHAPTER THREE

Brother

In the fall of 1989, I had not heard from my older brother Jimmy for many years. At this time, he was now thirty-seven years old. In fact, my two older sisters and my parents had not heard from him either. On my part, there was no lost love here in this relationship to even want to go and search for him. I can remember being only five or six years old, and as some older brothers notoriously do, he would beat up on me for no apparent reason. When the day was done, in many instances, what he instigated got blamed on me and more often than not, I was the one put in the dog house. There was no justice! That early-on pouncing was basically the dynamic of our relationship that lasted until he moved away from the house at the age of eighteen. In 1989 he was out of sight and therefore the pain of it all was out of mind. But that was about to change.

On a Wednesday night in October of 1989, I was fast asleep, when all of a sudden I had a terrifying dream about my brother. It was so horrible; it moved me to feel compassion for him. Something I don't ever recall having before for this angry soul. In the dream, I saw my brother in an empty and very dimly lit room. Of all places, he was lying on the floor. He had no bed and no possessions. Instantly, I became acutely aware that he was suffering greatly, that he was dying and most terrifying of

Proof of the *Afterlife* – *The Conversation Continues*

all, he was dying alone. In the dream, I was aware that he had no friends, no family and no one to come to his aid.

As we all do, upon awakening, I dismissed this dream as something connected to the crazy world of nocturnal imaginings. I blocked out its content and went on my merry way of work and activities for the day. *"No one believes that God converses this way - do they?"* I thought to myself. Well, that denial did not last for long.

It was now the very next night, Thursday, and while I was fast asleep, it was if I had gone to a movie theater and the entire vision from the night before was played over again in its entirety. I saw the same stark, dimly lit room, and my brother lying on the floor. Again, I was acutely aware that he was suffering so, but had no one to assist him or even care about him.

Upon awakening, I had a sense that God was talking to me and I needed to listen. The first thing I did was to contemplate the "what if." What if the two consecutive nights of dreams are true? Would I be willing to step in and be his friend? Would I be willing to be forgiving and compassionate, putting aside our differences? Out of nowhere, and in very little time, I had made the decision to help someone who at one time was considered the "enemy." Interiorly, it just seemed like the right thing to do. But how would I find him to see if everything was okay?

Immediately that same day, I telephoned an older sister who was living in Colorado at the time. I shared with her the content of the dream. She concurred that it would be a good idea to research this more. She thought of a friend in New York City that just may know something about Jimmy's whereabouts. Within a few days, she had received word that her friend had found our brother in Saint Francis hospital with a very critical condition – pneumonia for the third time in six months. Wow! God was talking and he was using amazing means to associate with our family and to help us. Although the news was not good at all, it was encouraging to know that God had used a series of dreams to speak out and send help for a dying soul. More importantly, he did it in a way that it became *"my idea"* to help my brother, and not a command where I was boxed in and I had no choice in the matter. God always suggests through inspiration and in that process completely respects our free will. He is a *perfect* gentleman.

My sister flew to New York in December, helped close out Jimmy's apartment and he boarded a flight for Miami, where he would be closer to me and I could facilitate his care. Because of my willingness to help him, my brother told others that the sun sort of rose and set on me. That was embarrassing because I knew that I was nothing special. Our life-long antagonistic relationship was instantly set aright by a combination of my simple act of charity and a lot of suffering on his part. As I said earlier, God does not send suffering, but he uses it as needed to establish dialogue with us and each other here on earth.

It was at a Miami hospital in January of 1990 that my mother and father appeared there to meet their prodigal son for the first time in years. It was also here that he was diagnosed as being H.I.V. positive. In the hallway, outside the door of Jimmy's hospital room, hostilely my father said to me, *"Well, what do you expect? That is what God does to gay people like him."* At that point, it became clear to me; my brother was being hated and rejected by his very own father.

Unfortunately, my mother was trained to follow the "party" line, so although she had a strong devotion to God, and of course a mother's instinct is to never forsake her child, she was afraid to disagree and suffer dad's wrath. When I had asked for their financial help with his care, they refused. When asking for some of their personal time, they refused as well, on the grounds that, *"our church friends would not understand."* My poor brother was being despised and rejected by those closest to him, his own mother and father. But in my mind, to a certain extent that was okay – Jesus suffered rejection by some closest to him, so Jimmy was in good company.

It was astonishing for my dad, of all people, however, to behave this way when he himself was apparently hiding severe skeletons in his own closet that, oddly enough, he did not feel were that bad. In hindsight, all severe sin is bad and one type is no better and no worse than another – they just have different names. That should cause each of us to be honest with ourselves about our sinfulness and be compassionate towards others in their struggles, contradictions and brokenness.

Being alerted by God to care for my brother, to offer him charity, compassion and mercy may have repaired that relationship in eternity, but the conversation obviously got worse withy my mother and father. It seemed evident to me that here are two people that say they love God, go to church every Sunday, but in the big picture have their own blatant sins of power, being judgmental, hate and hypocrisy still dominating our familial relationships. The injustice of it all tugged at every fabric of my moral sensibility to forgive and forget. In their case, it took years before that could ever completely happen.

God's compassion and powerful conversation with me and my brother was astonishing. It became very clear to me one of the messages that God was sending, through Jimmy's life story, is that he loves all of his children equally, no matter if they are straight, gay, black, brown, adulterer, atheist or saint. In my brother's case, I was overwhelmed by the personal responsibility of God as he delivered on his word in the Bible where the Psalmist David wrote, *"For he will deliver the needy who cry out, the afflicted who have no one to help. He will take pity on the weak and the needy and save the dying when they're alone. He will rescue them from oppression and violence, for precious is their blood in his sight."* (Psalm 72:12-14)

My brother died peacefully in his sleep in July of 1990. When he was buried, by my prompting, he had these words placed on his grave stone: *"Jesus said . . . 'Let us rejoice and be glad, because this brother of yours who was dead and is now alive again; he was lost and now is found.'"*

About two months after his death, in September of 1990, I can recall a vision where God permitted me, for the first time, the opportunity to visit my brother in the afterlife. What we shared together at that time was significant. In it, I was transported in spirit to the backyard of the large three story redbrick home that Jimmy and I grew up in as children. Immediately, I recognized my brother having a party at a picnic table under the shade of a grand old elm tree that our family loved. Spunky, he looked and acted as if he was fourteen. He and a few friends (who were deceased too) were having a good time talking, eating and playing in the yard as if they were teenagers again. I asked him if he was okay, he said *"Yes!"* and that he was very happy. With that, I was satisfied that he was doing well, I turned around, left him and returned back to my body.

After pondering the vision on and off for many years, it occurred to me that the place we refer to as "Purgatory" may have many and various levels, as well as many and different purposes for developing a soul before it can enter into heaven. In my brother's case, he was given an opportunity to grow and mature through some years of his life that he missed out on. The intensity of childhood abuse that was present in our family, especially from my father, had robbed him of some key formative years. Now, through the love and mercy of God, he was being given a chance to mature through what was lost through no fault of his own. God is enormously responsible for the abuses that occur within his creation. He was calling my brother to be his son and he was providing for him an afterlife dialogue and an association that would mature him and prepare him for heaven. God is amazing, and he is doing these astonishing things in our lives that very few people believe and will give him credit for; namely his steadfast love, mercy and compassion that unites us to himself as his conversation continues with each of us, no matter what – even after death!

In 2008, almost three years after my NDE, I had an encounter with my brother for a second time in the afterlife. This time, instead of it being a vision, he came directly to me while I was asleep and spoke with me initially in the form of an interior locution. A locution is a word, or two, or a phrase that a person may receive, establishing a conversation with God, saints or from others in the afterlife that are in heaven or purgatory. In the 1500s, Saint Teresa of Avila received many, and said there are three types of locutions; the hearing of a voice speaking interiorly, hearing a voice speaking audibly, or having a sudden but profound thought. Here is what I wrote in my journal about this second encounter with my brother in the afterlife:

Wednesday, May 28, 2008 – This morning, while I was asleep, I received an interior locution where in it my brother began conversing with me about my acoustical guitar playing at church. He said, *"I like it when you sing the song, 'To you Yahweh, I lift up my Soul, O my God.'"* Right then and there, I sang the song for him, passing a few minutes together. He listened intently and then I was given the gift to also see him visually and the great amount of happiness and joy the serenade brought him.

After this time together, I was not clear in my own mind as to whether my brother was as of yet to arrive in heaven. But one thing was for sure, he had matured greatly from where he was in 1990, just three months after his death. Now, in 2008 he was no longer a teenager. Because of his interest in heavenly songs and worship, I surmised that he was on the right track and definitely on his way to heaven. That would soon be confirmed in what happens next.

In the early morning hours of Wednesday, September 9, 2009 (9/9/9), my brother's birthday, I recorded this in my journal: Lord God, this morning, [not even realizing it was Jimmy's birthday until later in the day] you came to me and spoke … *"I took your brother to heaven today* [today] *because there was one time in his life when he was merciful to someone."* Next, you interiorly showed me how my brother, one day, went to a small New York neighborhood grocery store on Bleeker Street to buy food and water and then delivered it all compassionately to someone who really needed it. As a result of that one act of mercy, you also had mercy on him and took him to heaven.

My brother was not much known for his selflessness. Usually what we fought most about growing up was the fact that he would disappear when there were chores to be done around the house. Later, once he moved out of the house, he apparently got wrapped up, as so many do, into an *"it's all about me"* lifestyle, which included many parties, alcohol and drugs. While growing up, it was highly unusual for Jimmy to remember Mother's Day with a card or a family member's birthday. But of course he sure appreciated when we remembered his!

I share all of this not to make fun of his shortcomings, but to illustrate how big and how great God's mercy is toward each one of us. Jesus said, *"Blessed are the merciful, they shall obtain mercy."* (Matthew 5:7) Apparently, Jimmy's one and only selfless act of mercy toward another, paved the way for him to be welcomed into heaven after nearly twenty years in Purgatory. God's mercy is so much more extensive and vast than the way we see mercy and justice here on earth.

Some who have previewed this book before it went into print have read the story of my brother and have found it troubling – disconcerting. It seems implausible to some as to how a guy who had led a troubled, party and gay lifestyle in New York City winds up in heaven. However, it should not seem that unbelievable based on Jesus' parable of the "Laborers in the Vineyard." Here is the story, as it illustrates the unfathomable and bottomless mercy of God. Jesus turns conventional wisdom of justice upside down!

"For the kingdom of heaven is like a landowner who went out early in the morning to hire men to work in his vineyard. He agreed to pay them a denarius for the day and sent them into his vineyard. About the third hour he went out and saw others standing in the marketplace doing nothing. He told them, *'You also go and work in my vineyard, and I will pay you whatever is right.'* So they went. He went out again about the sixth hour and the ninth hour and did the same thing. About the eleventh hour he went out and found still others standing around. He asked them, *'Why have you been standing here all day long doing nothing?'* *'Because no one has hired us,'* they answered. He said to them, *'You also go and work in my vineyard.'* When evening came, the owner of the vineyard said to his foreman, *'Call the workers and pay them their wages, beginning with the last ones hired and going on to the first.'* The workers who were hired about the eleventh hour came and each received a denarius. So when those came who were hired first, they expected to receive more. But each one of them also received a denarius. When they received it, they began to grumble against the landowner. *'These men who were hired last worked only one hour,'* they said, *'and you have made them equal to us who have borne the burden of the work and the heat of the day.'* But he answered one of them, *'Friend, I am not being unfair to you. Didn't you agree to work for a denarius? Take your pay and go. I want to give the man who was hired last the same as I gave you. Don't I have the right to do what I want with my own money? Or are you envious because I am generous?'* So the last will be first, and the first will be last." (Matthew 20:1-16)

There is a case similar to my brother's in a book called *"Get Us Out Of Here!"* The book is about an Austrian mystic by the name of Maria Simma who recently passed away at the age of eight-nine on March 16, 2004. By the time of her death, Maria had conversed with hundreds of souls from Purgatory since 1940 when the visitors first began to call on her at the age of twenty-five. One soul in particular appeared to Maria Simma asking for prayers that might help her to go to heaven one day. Simma offered to pray for her and then asked her to share a bit about herself. The woman explained that she almost wound up in hell because of the awful self-centered life she had lived. However, last minute, God was merciful to her because of *one* act of kindness that she genuinely had performed.

As the story goes . . . One day, while leaving the front door of her home and going off on her way to work, she looked at the house next door and remembered that an elderly sick woman lived there. So, she knocked on the door and offered to go to the store and to help out the old woman. As a result of that one act of mercy and compassion, upon her death, she was given mercy in her own hour of need and at the very last minute. She won herself a spot in Purgatory with the hope of one day going to heaven.

Shortly before her death, Maria Simma was asked in an interview for Canadian-based *Michael* magazine, *"Maria, why does one go to Purgatory? What are the sins which most lead to Purgatory?"* She replied, *"Sins against charity, against the love of one's neighbor, hardness of heart, hostility, slandering, and calumny* [lies] — *all these things."* Our sins against charity are all our rejections of certain people we do not like, our refusals to make peace, our refusals to forgive, and all the bitterness we store inside.

Yes, the conversation is going on all around us. Ultimately, it is God's good will and good pleasure to upright all wrongs, and to bring about reconciliation by establishing a dialogue with him and healthy relationships with each other; whether a person is dead or alive, it doesn't matter.

Reconciliation is not an easy thing to do. You have to be God to unravel, and untangle all the wrongs that are going on around us and in us; in the past, present and future. All the evil and all the bad that have ever been done; God has a silent but profound plan to reconcile all things harmoniously back into himself. As Isaiah once wrote . . . *"Comfort, comfort my people, says your God. Speak tenderly to Jerusalem, and proclaim to her that her hard service has been completed, that her sin has been paid for, that she has received from the Lord's hand double for all her sins. A voice of one calling: 'In the desert prepare the way for the Lord make straight in the wilderness a highway for our God. Every valley shall be raised up, every mountain and hill made low; the rough ground shall become level, the rugged places a plain. And the glory of the Lord will be revealed, and all mankind together will see it. For the mouth of the Lord has spoken.'"* (Isaiah 40:1-5)

CHAPTER FOUR

Father

In August of 1999, I had written a *"can we talk"* letter to my father, Jim Sr. (my brother was known as "Jimmy" or Jim Jr.) and I sent a copy of the letter to my mother as well. She never received it because my dad, who got the mail each day, pulled a "KGB" and was monitoring what she read. The letter was in response to a recent phone conversation with my mom where she aired her tearful concerns that in their latter retirement years, he was still very angry and verbally aggressive toward her and for no apparent reason. Some hardened people soften in their old age, but at this juncture, at the age of eighty-two, not my dad! In one phone call in particular, mom was lamenting that a simple change of the house thermostat setting to higher or lower, would set him off in an argumentative rage.

When I sent my letter to him in the blazing heat of August, I suggested that a life-time of belligerent behavior had to stop. In opening, I quoted from a letter his youngest daughter had written him a few weeks earlier, which my sister had shared with me. In it she said, *"This principle of 'know it all' – 'superiority' – 'right at any price' permeates so many areas of your mind.* [It permeates] *your daily ways of functioning and responding to everything that there is no single answer* [for your unreasonable and ill behavior toward others]. Her point was well made and I concurred with her assessment and frustration.

As my letter progressed, I defended my mother and said many of the things that she found difficult to say. Especially, because for her it would have been a politically bad move to confront him (or so she thought) for fear she would wind up out on the street unable to fend for herself in her old age. In part, this is what I said, *"Although mom is extremely unhappy in her present day marital situation with you, she feels that your anger, rudeness, belligerent attitude, and at times violent shouting matches, is related to your prescription medication. In some respects she feels obligated to be a victim of spouse abuse because of your health problems and she feels that your medications are further driving your ill behavior."*

After recapping a long history of other severe abuses, I assured him that the intention of my letter was not to belittle him, but to offer love and forgiveness – but he must fess up and make an effort to change. About midway through, I said: *"Your horrible behavior continued well into my teens and twenties* [with no letting up]. *I have forgiven you and love you. I am only saddened that you continue to behave poorly toward the only person left in the house, your wife – to this very day."* My one sister, (the younger of the two) was not as forgiving or understanding, and still may not be to this very day, and for good reason. She had been badly hurt by him and my mother's denial of the damage he was causing.

Lastly, the letter had a call to conversion; to choose life and to offer him final assurances of love and forgiveness. I closed with the following words . . .

"[Dad] *if you are ready to do some things differently starting today – then let us all be friends. If you are willing to forgive as we have forgiven you, then begin today to live in the spirit of friendship, equality and family. Shed your anger and abuse and choose peace.*

"My hope is that you will choose life, the Spirit, forgiveness and happiness over the darkness and the argumentative behavior that you have perpetrated and has shrouded your marriage and family for years. It's never too late to blossom. Spring always comes. Let a decision to personally change and be a kinder and gentler man bring renewal and create something wonderfully beautiful to take with you into your next life.

"We your children wouldn't mind an apology, but we're not waiting for one. More importantly mom is waiting for something she said you have never said – 'I'm sorry.' You have never said that to her! She said those two simple words up to now have not been in your vocabulary. Please make a determination now to become a kinder person and a better listener . . . You will always be loved and forgiven by Christ's example. (Signed) . . . Your Loving Son."

Of course this is a book about conversation. Sometimes the conversation may be uncomfortable, difficult and even painful to engage in, as it was here. As life gets more entangled and goes awry, people are less likely to have dialogue for that very reason. Forgiveness, kindness, mercy and compassion are the keys that open up the dialogue door in tough times and in difficult situations like these, but not always instantly. However, many cannot see how charitable qualities are productive, so they run from kindness and compassion and things only get worse. Then they become more angry, spiteful, unkind and unforgiving. In August of 1999 when I spoke to a parish priest about my letter and the fact that it was ill received, he said, *"Your problem is that you and your sisters waited entirely too long to have this conversation."*

Yes, the letter was ill received. In short, my father denied everything and permanently cut off contact with all three of his remaining children. My mom never saw the letter so she only heard his side of the story. Ultimately backing him up, she became a temporary accomplice in his divisive tactic to sever dialogue with us and followed him into denial and silence. That would later change when a few months after his death God supernaturally descended upon my mother and showed her everything my father had done, and then some. Her eyes were opened and she grieved for years after. I will share more about that in Chapter 5 titled, *Mother.* Dad died in my mother's arms four years after my letter. He passed from a sudden burst of an aneurism shortly after 8:00am on the morning of July 14, 2003.

At his death, I stuck by my letter of forgiveness and that made it possible for me to attend his funeral and wish him well. However, just saying *"I forgive"* is one thing, but really knowing-that-you-know you have forgiven is another. It is here that God stepped in and energized the conversation just about two years after my father's death.

As I said in Chapter 2, by September of 2005, I had been attending daily Mass and Communion for a few weeks and had also begun to daily read the Scriptures once again. Over this time period, I became more contemplative. Thoughts began to occur to me that a complete interior forgiveness of my father was absolutely possible just by recognizing the fact, *"I am a sinner too!"* *"My failures and shortcomings are just different from his,"* I surmised. Everyone's particular brand of sins may have different names but the same end – self-destruction. That realization within my own heart motivated me to revisit forgiveness and make it complete once and for all.

With that said, the contradictions and hypocrisy going on with my dad and mom, I later had the ability to constructively frame and explain this way . . . It seems to me that it does not much matter whether one's severe, unrepented sin, is as big as the gash in the haul of the Titanic or a hole the size of a baseball, in either case that person is going down with the ship (hell). It also seems, now more than ever, many well-meaning religious people find it easy to take judgmental pot shots at minorities like drug addicts, homeless, alcoholics, prostitutes, obese and gay people to mention a few – all the while, many who are married are cheating at one time or another (about 60%) on their own spouses, because it's more septic as long as one does not get caught, and thanks be to God, it's considered "straight sex." Yet, even still, others are secretly stealing from employers, lusting in their hearts (adultery) and turning their homes and cars into consuming money pits (idolatry), all of which are violations of the Ten Commandments. In America today, for some reason, these "majority-type sinners," apparently, do not see the log that is in their own eye. All the while they hate "minority-type sinners"– individuals who are struggling with their own, very unique brand of addictions, sins, problems and issues. "Majority-type sinners" seem to be concerned about removing the spec from others' eyes, while ignoring their own contradictions and brokenness. Jesus, undeniably, condemns religious hypocritical behavior of this sort and frequently speaks out against it in the Gospels.

Henri Nouwen, in his acclaimed book, *The Return of the Prodigal Son,* asks the question, *"Which offense is more identifiable to sinners, lust or self-righteousness?"* In chapter six, Nouwen asserts that in Jesus' parable of the Prodigal Son, the younger son is swept away by lust, greed and is wickedly wasteful. The elder son, although he is obedient and dutiful, he is swept away by the darkness of selfishness, pride and bitter arrogance.

Recently, www.HomelessInAmerica.BlogSpot.com bloggers, were polled a poignant question inspired by Nouwen. They were asked, *"In your opinion, which sin is more readily identifiable and easily repented for, lust or self-righteousness?"* According to the readers, it appears as though the lustfully poor, the broken and the morally bankrupt seem to have an intuitive clarity that their lust is sin. However, the wealthy-powerful-self-righteous, in the opinion of the readers, may have an absence of right moral judgment about themselves and their sin. The vast majority of our bloggers - 95% felt that the offense of lust is most easily identified by sinners. Only a miniscule group - 5% felt that the sin of self-righteousness is most easily identified and repented for.

The Apostle Paul was no stranger to the evil of self-righteousness and hypocrisy. Paul confronted it when he said, *"You, then, who teach others, do you not teach yourself? You who preach against stealing, do you steal? You who say that people should not commit adultery, do you commit adultery?"* Romans 2:21-22 If Paul were alive today, possibly he would add . . . *"You who condemn others that have sex addictions, or who are dependent on drugs and alcohol; are you yourself cheating on your spouse, being a workaholic or shopaholic, abusing prescription medications or do you have another weakness or sin that you hide from others?"*

Ultimately, this type of judgmental behavior by church members comes at a cost and it comes with a warning from Paul. He wrote, *"You, therefore, have no excuse, you who pass judgment on someone else, for at whatever point you judge the other, you are condemning yourself, because you who pass judgment do the same things. Now we know that God's judgment against those who do such things is based on truth. So when you, a mere man, pass judgment on them and yet do*

the same things, do you think you will escape God's judgment?"
Romans 2:1-4

But, I digress. Let's get back to the story about my father. Because of this complete forgiveness of my dad that had interiorly taken place, in the days leading up to my NDE of September 27th, I was beginning to experience waves of intense peace and joy that would flood my inner being. At strange moments in time – for instance while driving the car or taking a walk, I would all of a sudden become "drunk" with laughter and joy. I was learned enough in Holy Scripture to know that I was experiencing the fruits of the Holy Spirit. God was all over me.

The conversation is getting ready to intensify. In November of 2005, just a few weeks after the NDE I was fast asleep for the night when all of a sudden at 4:00am I was overcome by a strange event. Here is what I noted in my journal:

Friday, November 18, 2005 – In the early hours of yesterday morning, startled, I suddenly awoke at 4:00am. While having been solidly asleep, I heard a loud voice crying out like a broadcast over a megaphone's loudspeaker. The voice said, *"Your father is very proud of you and your mother!"* Instantly awake, I sat up in bed and saw a figure, one resembling my father, standing right in front of me. It was him, but hardly recognizable because he was shrouded in black. He was wearing black pants and a black shirt. His arms and skin were black too. For a few seconds, he looked intently at me but was unable to speak. Next, I had an interior locution that he was proud of me and my mom because of our Faith as well as our daily commitment to Mass and Communion. To my astonishment, early Friday morning (today) while I was fast asleep, the scenario happened all over a second time.

In a phone call today, I shared with my mother the two back-to-back visions and locutions. I was hesitant at first. What would she think? However once shared, they echoed as being authentic to her because she said that dad had never once mentioned he was proud of her or the children in all the 63 years they were married. She had a strong reaction of emotion and tears hearing the words spoken possibly by a Guardian Angel on his behalf, *"Your father is very proud of you and your mother."* As she profusely sobbed, she said, *"He finally gets it after all these years, after he is dead and gone!"*

For days after, I contemplated the meaning of all of this and then the thought occurred to me, *"My dad must be in Purgatory!"* It seemed to make sense because he was shrouded in black as well as the fact that he could not speak for himself. Apparently his Guardian Angel or another angel had to do the speaking for him. At any rate, shrouded in black, and mute silence could not be good and it was evidence enough that he needed our prayers. I consulted with my Spiritual Director, Fr. F. and he recommended that my mom and I begin to offer prayers and Masses for him. But there was much more that

God had in store as the healing; the forgiveness and the conversation of our family ensued.

Inspired by an interior waking locution from the Lord in late November of 2005, I quickly set my sights on becoming a volunteer to serve the homeless. In Los Angeles at that time, there were more than 90,000 homeless men, women, children and teens living under bridges, in alleyways and on the streets of the city. But I did not know how to "break into the business" of caring for poor homeless souls. A few days later, on a Saturday morning while on a day retreat at my church, a woman sitting right next to me was of all things, vice-president of one of the largest homeless agencies in downtown. It was just three blocks from where I lived. What are the chances? Within a few days, she had me scheduled for an interview with one of the managers of the organization by the name of Angelina. The interview went well and I was accepted as a volunteer job placement counselor. I received my own office and began to work twenty hours a week from 8:00am to 12:00 noon, Monday through Friday. However, Angelina was not your "normal" supervisor.

After only a couple days of work at the homeless center, Angelina stopped by my office, she looked up to the center of the room and alarmingly shouted, *"Jim, Jim!"* Not even looking at me, abruptly, she left as fast as she came in with no explanation. She repeated that same scenario again, later that same morning. *"Jim, Jim!"* she shouted for yet a second time.

The next morning upon arriving back to work, she poked her head through my office door and asked me to immediately come see her at her desk. She shut the door of her office and explained that she is a Christian mystic and that yesterday she saw a spirit in my office – twice in fact. *"His name is Jim,"* Angelina blurted out without hesitation. She called out to *"Jim"* hoping to distract the invasion because she thought he might be disturbing me. *"So, who's dead in your family by the name of Jim?"* she said authoritatively. Speechless, I stuttered for words. *"Oh, well uh, my brother who passed away in 1990 is Jim and my father who died in 2003 is Jim as well. Both have the name of Jim,"* I replied. *"He wasn't young!"* she emphatically said. Angelina continued, *"It was an older man and therefore it had to be your father."* From what she witnessed, he was intently watching me – curious about my work with the poor and seemed to want to get to know me – something he had not done very well while here on earth.

Well, the conversation was heating up and now I had hard evidence – even a manager and co-worker had become a neutral and credible eyewitness to what God was doing in our family's lives. Obviously, Angelina had no way of knowing about my dad because we had just met two days earlier and purely by way of a professional interview. It would have been impossible for her to know about the auditory locution and appearance of my dad just a few weeks earlier. That was private information and no one knew about it but me and my mother at that early stage. But there is way more to this story. God had much more to do connecting the disconnected!

In the early morning hours of July 20, 2006, just about eight months after the experience I had with Angelina, another significant event took place. Here is how I recorded the morning in my journal:

Thursday, July 20, 2006 – I just awoke with my heart pounding as if I had run a race. First, I remember suddenly leaving my body, exiting through a penthouse apartment bedroom window and then having a birds-eye view high above downtown and the skyscrapers. Next, I began to pass through many small rooms deep in the earth constructed of very thick cement walls. The well-built construction of each reminded me of rooms having been fashioned in the style of bomb shelters. After being transported in spirit through a few rooms with great difficulty, I became fearful that I would become stuck and never would be able to return back to my body. At that thought, I turned back around and began to leave. Next, the same Jesus that held me at the time of my NDE came ever so gently along side of me. He said, *"You can do it if you have faith."* Yes, I had faith, I knew I did and immediately I became stronger. By trusting in Christ, I was able to descend swiftly and smoothly through many more layers of rooms constructed of these thick cement walls, but this time it was as if they were made of thin air. I had no more fear of them, especially knowing that the Lord was there. When I arrived however, I was alone. The room was very small, dimly lit, foggy and desolate. Immediately I saw my father who had died three years earlier, almost to the day, seated at a very small café table. Quite naturally, taking him by the hand, I made an invitation to him and said, *"Come, stand aside so we could talk."* My conversation with him was centered on the questions, *"Had Christ come to console you since your death? Had he appeared to you yet?"* I said. He shook his head, *"No."* He looked very introspective and despondent.

While I was still speaking with my father, a gentle man entered the room from around a dimly lit corner in front of me and to my left. He was like an angel, a soft low light glowed from his face and he appeared peaceful and confident. He gave me a nod of calm assurance. Possibly he was my father's Guardian Angel; he appeared to be an attendant from the Lord who was there to help my dad, myself and our family. I looked at the angel and said, *"The peace of Christ be with you."* Without speaking, it seemed as though we were both there on a similar mission – to console my father. Having the assurance that my dad was in good hands, I immediately turned around and felt the liberty to return through the very same solid walls from which I had come. I arrived in my bedroom and instantly awoke. My heart was pounding as if I had run a marathon.

After some reflection this morning, it is safe to say my father is in Purgatory and in an aspect of it that is very isolating – similar to solitary confinement. The rooms found in this part of Purgatory are very small, constricting, devoid of comforts and intimacy. The intensely thick walls and imprisonment leaves

Proof of the *Afterlife – The Conversation Continues*

one feeling captive and desolate. Without the soul having had charity and a living Faith in God while on earth, one may lack the power to call on Christ and to be freed from the darkness that overwhelms them here. The darkness and isolation is suffocating. (Purgatory appears to be designed so that one's conversation with God somehow continues on his terms, and with his methods, to purge us of our faithlessness, as well as our unmerciful, unforgiving and selfish ways.)

Not long after this, I remember Fr. F. posing a question that I had not thought much about. He said, *"Do you think God will let you know when your dad finally gets out of Purgatory?"* That was a great question, but I never really thought much more about it until February of 2008. Here is what I recorded one afternoon in my journal:

Saturday February 2, 2008 – On this day at 1:30pm, what I thought would be a short afternoon nap, immediately the power of you O God, fell upon me. God the Father, your powerful and loving presence mightily overshadowed me in my room. You weighed heavily upon me as I remained crushed and immobilized by your awesome and Holy Presence. Then, you brought into the room and presented my own father. He was incredibly strong and radiantly different from when I had seen him in Purgatory, on July 20, 2006. Today I saw him as he is now in heaven, and how you intend each of us to be – whole, complete, happy, smiling and joyful and in perfect unity with you.

Next, I remember Jesus entering through the door of my room and then coming from behind me. He placed his arm around me and my father, as if to say, *"Everything is fine now, I have reconciled you and your father and all things in your life. Peace be with you."* Coming out of a suspended state, I came to after the apparition had ended, filled with tears of happiness for my father. I was overflowing with joy to see his completeness. I rejoiced to see the mercy that was shown my father by you, God my Father.

CHAPTER FIVE

Mother

As my mother Paula tells her story, in October of 2003, just about three months after my father's death, she had arrived home as usual at eleven o'clock in the morning after having attended daily Mass, Communion and sharing coffee and freshly baked bread rolls with the "church ladies" at a local café. This was her daily habit for the past fifty years. Since the 1960s, when I was in grade school, I can remember her going to morning Mass, and then crossing the nearby railroad tracks to volunteer as a substitute teacher at my elementary school. However, on one tranquil and mild fall day in 2003, there was nothing serene about what would happen next.

Upon walking in the house and placing her car keys down on the kitchen counter, she was instantly overcome by an interior revelation powered by the Holy Spirit, as she tells it, illuminating her conscience and mind. It seemed as though all her years of going to daily Mass, and praying the rosary, had placed her on God's radar to receive special graces and help. What she learned next, was going to be one of those profound days, that in hindsight, although turbulent, it would become a valuable gift from the Lord.

In a very brief moment of time, she became intensely aware that all the accusations floating around the family regarding her husband were true, and then some. Simultaneously she received a locution and the words, *"He did it all."* In an instant, she was enlightened like a dry desert soaking up the springtime rains. Believe me, for my mother to be able to face the truth had to be the work of God. To admit any flaws went against the "white picket fence" image she and my father desperately tried to keep up over the years. Together, they held the fundamental world view, *"the world is wrong, but we're right."* It's akin to the transactional analysis expert, Thomas Harris' book, *I'm OK, You're OK*, and his profound identification of the disorder, *"I'm OK, you're not OK,"* world view.

As sweet as my mom was, and yet with her head in the sand most of the time, my mother was a person who frequented church, tuned out everyone else, and strangely, indulged in playing Bingo and gambling trips to Las Vegas, all the while believing everything her husband told her, never questioning a word he said. Jokingly, family and friends often said they were the original "Edith" and "Archie" from the television sitcom, *"All in the Family."* None of us children would have ever thought in a million years that she would escape her narrow-minded world of self-denial and self-centeredness, except by an act of God. And an act of God it was. The conversation was heating up for her.

She immediately picked up the phone and called my eldest sister. Surprisingly, for the first time in her life, she was able to verbalize and discuss some of the abuse my dad perpetrated and covered up over the lifetime of our family. Also, she became acutely aware that some trips to Las Vegas with my dad were not just innocent or petty gambling vacations – especially because there were times that he disappeared from the hotel and gave no explanation or apology for his hours of mysterious absence. A simple, two-plus-two, made a solid four, and boy was she fuming, raging mad in fact and feeling betrayed! But knowing the truth is the first step to embracing forgiveness isn't it? God wanted to give her a heavy dose of the truth. Most importantly, he wanted the truth to be known in order to challenge her ability to grant forgiveness as Jesus forgave his executioners on the Cross.

Even on the telephone, I knew she was extremely upset by the tone of her voice. Because, on call after call, she repeatedly and angrily vented to me about dad over these past six years, leading up to her recent death a few months ago. Just when I thought mom had resolved everything, six months later, she would rehash the same wounds and unforgiveness toward dad. Her profuse crying made it clear that she was hurt, abused and feeling deceived. In fact, just a few weeks ago, after a one-year battle with breast cancer, upon her death, I noticed something odd about some of the family photos in the house. In picture after picture she had ripped off the part with my dad standing next to her. She had been crazy mad, and for good reason. But could she forgive?

Heaven is only for people that know how to forgive, and because of her bout with terminal cancer in 2009-2010, she had to make some fast decisions about such matters before passing on to the next life. To facilitate her forgiveness of my dad, God granted her an additional miracle about one year before her death. Because God knows the future – he knew the soon coming date of her death. He also had decided to step up the conversation in order to get her ready for heaven. Here is what I wrote it in my journal:

———————————

Thursday, April 3, 2009 – Lord, in your mercy, last night you granted my mother and me back-to-back companion visions with my father appearing from the afterlife in order to bring about some forgiveness on her part that may be long overdue. In the encounter, my father came to me and lamented, *"Your mother is still mad at me and she is still complaining about me after all these years."* He asked for my help. My candid response to him was, *"Dad, don't worry, that is just the way she is, she doesn't mean anything by it. Besides, you know how women are; sometimes they may hold a grudge for a long while. Give her time, she will get over it."* (Now, if you are a woman reading this, please do not hold this dialogue against me. I am only journaling what I spontaneously constructed within the context of an afterlife conversation.)

Now, today, while speaking with my mother by phone about a different matter (I was not planning to discuss the above encounter with her) she excitedly quipped, *"Oh, by-the-way, I had a dream about your father last night."* I responded, *"I did too! Tell me all about yours first and then I'll tell you mine."* *"Well,"* she said, *"As soon as I saw him, I began complaining to him about all the things he did to me in our marriage of over sixty some years and I was very mad at him. I told him get the hell out of here!"*

After mom finished, I said to her again, *"I had a dream about dad last night too!"* Her response was, *"Okay, tell me about it."* Then I proceeded to share with her the content of what I wrote above. It was obvious, the whole situation was now adding up to each of us having had a direct encounter with my father in the hereafter. My meeting with him obviously took place right after he had just visited with my mother. She was silent and dumbfounded by it all, but God was speaking.

And so, Lord, as a result of the companion back-to-back dreams, it opened up dialogue with my mom about your mercy and how we are obligated to share your mercy with others. We discussed how God often gives certain individuals longer lives on this earth, in order for them to freely choose complete forgiveness, compassion, mercy and understanding of those who have hurt them in this life. Every day we wake up, it's one more additional day on earth that we have to make a decision to be forgiving of others and to make right and bring to order our relationships.

With all that said, I have to back up a little. Being kindhearted to the poor and the broken was historically difficult for my mother practically her entire life. Now, all of a sudden seeing her very own husband whom she naively held up for sixty-three years as a wealthy "superstar," he was now "poor" and broken too. It was not going to be easy to be merciful to him or anyone else in this pitiable condition. She had little experience being sympathetic to the poor. Her faith in God gave her a lot of practice praying and seeking after him, but somehow she missed out on many of the pastors' homilies and Gospel lessons of forgiveness, compassion and mercy, to her own recent admission just weeks before her death. However, we know that there are but three things that last; faith, hope and love, and the greatest of these is love. (cf. 1 Corinthians 13:13)

We don't have to be theologians to know that patience, mercy and empathy for the poor is conditional to being authentically Christian. Jesus, within the first few days of his ministry, stood up in the synagogue and publicly declared his mission as one to the poor; not to the rich and powerful. The latter were the ones that he knew one day would crucify him. On this particular day, he read from the scroll of Isaiah and then said he was the fulfillment of its message. Jesus read, *"The Spirit of the Lord is on me, because he has anointed me to preach good news to the poor. He has sent me to proclaim freedom for the prisoners and recovery of sight for the blind, to release the oppressed, to proclaim the year of the Lord's favor."* (Luke 4: 18-19)

My mother is a wonderful person, don't get me wrong. But if she judged you as "lazy," such as a homeless guy, a poor person or a certain racial minority that she stereotyped as slothful – well you get the picture . . . Someone she pegged this way, could potentially drown and die before she would throw out a donation or a "life jacket" in the form of compassion or a even dollar bill to them.

Mom's predicament of struggling to integrate a strong prayer life along with the pure virtues of mercy and compassion is not uncommon. Her story reminds me of a couple of daily Mass-going "church ladies" who a few years ago cornered me at a local restaurant and said, *"We decided we don't want to be a part of your prayer group!"* I said, *"Oh, why is that?"* *"Well we heard that it is primarily going to be a way to help the homeless,"* they replied. *"And here's the point,"* they said. *"We're both immigrants. When we came to this country we hardly had clothes on our backs. We started out with nothing. We worked hard for the nice houses and cars we have today. The homeless are just lazy bums!"* What can you say to that? I was speechless and remained silent.

After my NDE, mom occasionally discussed, out of curiosity, my work with the homeless, especially those living under bridges and in remote alleyways. She was frequently perplexed by it all and had a lot of sometimes unkind and edgy questions about these poor and broken souls. Every few months, just when you think all her concerns had been addressed, she would be right back to square one and say something like, *"But aren't they lazy? Why don't they go out and get a job and work for a living like your father did?"* After the past three – four years of this, it seemed as though there was no way of making sense with her on the matter of integrating her awesome prayer life with compassion for the poor. But with

God, all things are possible. Before her death, here is how God miraculously initiated that very important dialogue with her:

Tuesday, January 1, 2008 – Just as I was about to awaken, I received a profound locution from the Lord. *"I am going to give your mother wisdom,"* Jesus said. Instantly, I had an intense interior awareness that my mom is going to be blessed very soon with a strong spiritual wisdom and insight that she has never had before. Thank you Jesus!

It was now almost three years after my NDE and I had a track record of many visitations and locutions from the other side that were right on target. By now, I had a strong sense that when God speaks, something Big, with a capital "B" is going to happen. But because God is God, we can never really know how he is going to act or fulfill his words. I had to just wait and see.

I did not have to wait very long. Just a couple of weeks later, and right at the time of my mother's ninetieth birthday, two significant events happened to her to bring about the promised wisdom from on High. The first was on January 21, 2008. On this day she was supernaturally overcome by the physical presence of Christ when she received Communion one weekday Mass at her church. She described the event to me this way: *"I was walking up to receive the Host when all of a sudden I no longer saw the priest. I no longer saw anybody. A man appeared at my right side, put his arm around me and* whispered, *'I love you darling.'* *I don't remember taking the Host and I don't remember walking back to my seat. I was at peace, in another world."* In that instant, she became an eyewitness to the risen Christ. That touching from Jesus had a profound effect on her – weeping and grieving for her sins was one of them. That's how I know it was Christ who had appeared to her at that Communion rail. She became more docile, more peaceful and thereafter, she would even send $50 or $100 to help the homeless! But there is more.

Also, around this same time period, within a few days of the above episode, she had a direct and enlightening encounter with an angel, in a Wal-Mart parking lot of all places. Over the past two years after it first happened, she would frequently retell the following story that I will share with you now. Often she recounted the event in tears, and yet, was filled with peace too. Here is what she told me . . .

"I was going to get a slice of pizza one evening at the place by the church. You know the one, the Italian restaurant in the Wal-Mart shopping plaza. I always check around me after parking the car to make sure there are no strangers lurking. I waited. I looked around and saw no one. As I opened the car door, immediately a young homeless man with a cute patch of hair under his lip was standing right next to my car door. I wasn't afraid, but I asked what he wanted. He said, 'My name is Billy. Maam, do you have a dollar?' I said to him, what do you want the dollar for? He replied, 'Maam, it's for the Spirit.' I said what do you mean 'it's for the spirit', you mean for spirits, like

alcohol? You want to go drinking? 'No Maam' he replied. 'It is for the Spirit.'" With that, she gave him the dollar bill (*Billy*) and he cordially walked her to the door of the pizza shop. As he opened the door for her, he said, *"Maam, you're a saint."*

   After having a slice of pizza, she exited the restaurant's front door and all of a sudden, what again seemed like out of nowhere, Billy came up on her right side and began to walk her to the car. She said to him jokingly, *"What's your problem? Do you want another dollar?"* He replied, *"No Maam."* He continued, *"Maam, you're a saint."* Next, at the car door, my mom said her goodbyes to Billy and asked if he came to this parking lot often. She then said, *"Will I see you again?"* *"No Maam,"* he replied, *"You will never see me again."* With that final exchange she got in the car, slammed the door shut, and turned around to back out. As she looked back, Billy, was no where to be found. He was instantly gone, and just as quickly as he had come into view. In hindsight, it's significant that this angel appeared as a homeless man isn't it? Only God could orchestrate that particular heavenly messenger to deliver that poignant message.

   Directly, because of the encounter with Billy, my mother began to be more generous to the poor. Also, she was at peace. She greatly increased her donation to a new church school building fund too. And as I said before, she began to send me donations each month for the "lazy" homeless. Stunningly, in her last weeks, she even began to grieve, for no unexplainable reason, for certain suffering homeless souls that she heard about from our homeless ministry. For instance, she would frequently weep for the poor homeless guy who was living on the streets, while enduring the scourge of weekly chemotherapy. Compassion welled up inside of her and empathy poured out for this man's pain, suffering and the fact he had no place to lay his head to better endure the pain. At this juncture in time (because of her soon death), my mother was, by God's help, absorbing spiritual truths of cosmic proportions. She was genuinely feeling sympathy for the poor and broken like she never had before.

Personally, the weeping and grieving in this regard was encouraging to see. It tells a story that here is a soul that is also seeing God. Because, when we see the poor, the discarded, the ignored, the despised and the rejected, we are on track to see God. You see, God experiences the same rejection as the poor, so he is one with them, in total solidarity! Despite his rich testimony in mountain grandeur, hazy beaches, glorious heavens and fluffy clouds, he is ignored, scorned and despised by many. Likewise, when God came to earth, he was despised and rejected and received more of the same treatment. So when someone like my mother is now able to grieve while "seeing" the poor, she is seeing God and therefore was immediately on her way to heaven, no doubt.

In validation of what was happening to my mom in this regard is Jean Vanier, the founder of l'Arche, an international network of communities for the mentally disabled. He has become an "expert" in seeing God in the poor and broken. John

Paul II once referred to l'Arche as, *"a dynamic and providential sign of the civilization of love."* In a radio interview with Lydia Talbot, Vanier once said, *"If you are blind to the poor, you become blind to God, and there is the mystery because the Word became flesh, became little, became crucified. We know He is hidden in the poor and the weak and the fragile and whatever you do to the weak, whatever you do to the hungry, the thirsty, you do unto Jesus. Then, there are those incredible words of Jesus, 'Whoever among you who welcomes one of these little ones, welcomes me.'"*

Obviously my mother was being prepared for heaven by having all these peculiar and other-worldly experiences leading up to the time of her death. God was orchestrating for her many gifts and graces that would prepare her soul to go directly to heaven on Sunday, February 21, 2010. That is the day she passed away of breast cancer at the age of ninety-two in the early morning hours.

On Sunday, January 17, 2010, my mother met her doctor right inside the church after Sunday Mass. It was there that the doctor told her that there was not anything more that could be done. *"It will just be a matter of time"* he said. She immediately called me with the news. She was distraught and yet resigned to the fact that moving on from this life and going to God is what she has longed for and prepared for all her life. The news was bittersweet.

That same afternoon, while getting dressed to go out with friends, I received a locution from the Lord. Here is how I recorded it in my journal:

Sunday, January 17, 2010 – Lord, *"In three weeks"* is what I heard you say this afternoon shortly after speaking with mom on the phone and receiving the news that she does not have much more time to live. [Indeed, it was exactly three weeks later that I left to go to mom's house to care for her in her final weeks. Miraculously, there was at this same time period an outpouring of donations from members of various churches. Everyone was coming together, sensing urgency for me to get to my mom. It was all happening at the same time without anyone ever talking to each other.]

I arrived at my mother's house on Sunday, February 7, 2010. We had her favorite pizza together and reminisced about the encounter with "Billy." Many friends were over visiting and it seemed like a party more than an upcoming funeral. I had no way of knowing that the next four weeks were going to be a speedy decline for my mother. I also had no way of knowing the final – final preparations that God was going to ask her to make in her life. As Fr. F. said, *"Apparently you are there to be her spiritual guide."* Deacon Peter from her church one day said, *"Brother, you are 'Jesus' for your mother. God is going to use you."* In all humility, yes, God did use me. But it is only because he came through with a lot of conversation to make me ready to do my job. It was miraculous what he did to help me be a better spiritual guide for my mother at this difficult time period of death and dying, when a soul is in great anguish. Here is what I wrote in my journal in this regard:

––––––––––––––––––

Tuesday, February 9, 2010 – In the early hours of the morning Lord, you appeared in my room and embraced me in my bed. The peace and the joy you give are amazing. Next you took me in your arms on an amazing journey into heaven. The colors Lord, the colors are spectacular. The sky was what I like to call "Mother Mary blue" and the clouds were perfectly fluffy and white. Then, you let me go and I could fly freely through the heavens. But sometimes I got carried away and I would fly too fast or felt like I was falling. It was here that you taught me to always say, *"Jesus I trust in you."*

––––––––––––––––––

The same morning that the temporary transportation to heaven took place; I shared with my mother the elated and amazing journey I had just taken. My spirits were high and I was at peace. I was now more than equipped to be a strong spiritual guide for the last days that we had together before she eventually slipped into a coma. I confidentially described to her the afterlife, some elements of heaven that I was personally aware of and what to expect when she gets there. She had no reason to fear, I said, but only one thing to say, *"Jesus I trust in you."* She was very comforted and agreed that she could say, *"Jesus I trust in you."* Mom was a devoted follower of these same words as they were promoted by Saint Faustina Kowlaska in her *Divine Mercy* revelation and as recorded in her diary as mentioned earlier.

Lastly, I would like to draw attention to the fact that God cares about bringing everyone into the conversation, including the unborn. My mother, for many weeks right prior to her death, had repeatedly been seeing a small, tiny baby appearing to her. I knew for a fact that she was authentically seeing the child, because, often we would be carrying on a rich and well thought out conversation verifying her sound mind, and then all of a sudden she would stop and say, *"There's that little baby again. It's right here in front of me."*

It took me some weeks of reflecting on this to receive inspiration as to who this baby was and why it was appearing to her. One day I just blurted out, *"Mom, do you know who the baby is?"* *"No!"* she said. *"That baby is the miscarriage you had way back in 1952!"* *"The baby is anxiously waiting to be with you so it can be with its mother and mature into full adulthood."* I replied. Astonished at the revelation she then replied, *"Yes, I think you're right!"*

Before I was born, my mother had a miscarriage at approximately four months term. She aborted quite suddenly and right in the house where she was living at the time. The doctor was concerned for her welfare and so he had to examine the remains to make sure nothing was left inside that may cause her problems later. Because of this post miscarriage analysis, there was never a formal burial for the child that I'm aware of.

Since that time no one has thought much more about the baby or discussed it until now. Personally, seeing the baby's love, compassion and initiative to track down its mother after all these years inspired me to pick a name for the baby, "Francis." So as of a few weeks ago, our family grew to include five children, not just the four that were normally known. This event makes me wonder who could ever think that voluntary abortion is a good idea. Obviously, from this encounter it's not. Choosing to kill poor unborn little ones is the wrong thing to do. Pre-born children, like the one my mother had, are real souls, and most importantly, they are very loving and devoted to their mothers, and one could only imagine, their fathers too.

Coincidentally, with no real planning in mind, I finalized this chapter about my mother on Sunday, May 9, 2010, Mother's Day.

Lastly, right before this book went to press, I spoke with my cousin Ronda, whom I had not personally been in touch with for more than thirty years. She had left a kind message of condolence for our family on my voice mail a few days after mom's death. It was now, six months later and I was finally getting a moment to return her call. Hearing my voice, elatedly, she said, *"You're going to think I'm crazy, but I heard from your mom a few weeks after she died."* Calmly, I replied, *"No I won't, I promise! Tell me what happened."* *"Well,"* she said. *"I spoke with your mom at length about two months before she had passed. She had called me to say that she was in the latter stages of cancer and would be gone soon. Concerned, I asked her to give me a sign after her death that she is okay* [in heaven]. *And do you know what she said?"* "Tell me," I replied, inquisitively. With great enthusiasm in her voice she said, *"Your mom immediately said, 'I'll break something in your house!'"* "And the point being?" I replied. Excitedly, Ronda continued . . . *"About two months after your mom's death. I was home alone watching television in the living room. It was ten o'clock at night. All of a sudden I heard a crash in the basement. When I investigated, I discovered a small box filled with many glass items had mysteriously fallen off a storage shelf. Everything in the box survived the fall, except one piece. One item was busted. Just as your mom had promised, 'something' broke letting me know that she is okay!"*

Chapter Six

Cousin

As I had mentioned in Chapter One, my cousin Kim was a favorite since childhood. She came from a military family, but in all reality she was not the "military brat" we often hear about. Her father, my uncle Ralph, was a Colonel Major in the Air Force and their family at one time was stationed in Thailand, as well as Washington, DC, among other places. She grew up with an international cosmopolitan flare. Her mother was my father's youngest sister. Kim was raised with all the charm and grace that one could expect to see in a medieval castle princess, not necessarily a modern American military household. Her long blonde hair, model physique and tasteful dresses, only enhanced her interior charm. As children, we rarely saw each other except on special occasions or an annual vacation.

Right after I had begun work on a Ph.D., in Law and Ethics at Duquesne University, in the early 80s, Kim and I had reconnected. At that time I received a call from Kim with an invitation to interview at a new company she had just joined in the New York area, PEOPLExpress Airlines. They were particularly interested in hiring managers who had no airline experience in order to groom them their way. Within a couple months of the interviews, Kim and I were not just cousins, but also founding managers and stock owners of one of the hottest and controversial non-union airlines in the history of the aviation industry. They provided us rich business skills training, under the tutorage of *In Search of Excellence* authors and business gurus, Tom Peters and Robert Waterman.

After a few years there, PEOPLExpress (PE) was purchased by *Continental Airlines* in the late 80s. We soon left PE, merging our talents, and began a successful upstart career job fair company and business consulting group. However, by the late 1990s, Kim had reunited with a high school sweetheart and relocated, in order to marry and start a home. We stayed in touch from time-to-time by phone and after her sudden run-in with lung cancer in July of 2005, we spoke frequently. I offered her my prayers and as I shared in Chapter 2, I began to go to daily Mass for both her and my health woes and our special intentions.

On a cold winter's day in December of 2005, I attended early morning Mass at the downtown Cathedral before the hustle and bustle of the day had begun. After receiving communion, I knelt down and began to pray about what I could say or share with my cousin Kim, when I make the few thousand mile journey to see her in a few weeks. What do you say to a person you deeply care about and who does not have much more time to live? Of course I had the details of my NDE to speak about. That was encouraging. But I was praying and asking the Lord what else could I say and how would I say it. Immediately after whispering that prayer, I heard the following locution. I did not know at the time what a locution was for, I was still ignorant and unaware of what these things were, until Fr. F. and I had spoken about it in the months to come.

———————————

Friday, December 30, 2005 – As I was kneeling and praying after Communion, I heard the following, [make known to Kim] *"I the Lord have seen the blue stone in the ring that you love to wear. I have seen its star in the middle. The blue in the ring is the sea of faithful witnesses that have followed me throughout the ages and that I have welcomed you into. The star in your ring is you shining brightly. I see your star. I see you! Do not fear, for in my mercy I have prepared a place for you. In my grace, I will keep you free from pain. Let this be a sign unto you, a shining diamond ring has been left at the foot of my altar to proclaim your brightness. This is the word of the Lord and my covenant with you is eternal."*

———————————

Within just a few seconds of this locution, I began to deny it ever happened. Up until now, whenever something like this happened, it was at nighttime. That somehow seemed to make it better or more believable for some strange reason. But this was broad daylight. In my mind I was thinking, *"There's no way I am going to tell Kim about this locution. Besides, I have not seen her in many years. Does she even have a blue ring on her hand with a star in the middle?"* Then I surmised, *"I will look like a fool if all this turns out to be a hoax, a product of my imagination!"* But overtime, I realized that part of the nature of doing God's business is the willingness to be a fool. In hindsight, now I'm okay with that. I'm a fool!

Well, it was no hoax. A few more brief seconds passed, Fr. Kevin, the celebrant of the Mass, stood at the altar with a bright shining diamond ring in his hand. Jokingly he said, *"One of you ladies is now throwing rings at me. I have up here* [holding it up] *a nice shiny diamond ring and someone just left it at the altar while receiving Communion. Please see me after Mass and I will return it to you."* At that, he abruptly went on with the closing prayer and blessing. Wow, God is amazing! His ways are so far above our ways. With the sudden appearance of the diamond ring, God confirmed the authenticity of him speaking to me right then and there.

In spite of seeing the diamond ring displayed at the altar, I still had a very oh-so-slight tinge of doubt that this was God at work. (It's amazing how cold we humans have become; our minds seem to want to deny God is having a conversation, rather than readily embrace it.) As a result, I had no plans to call Kim and discuss the event with her. However, that same day, out of the clear blue, Kim called me in the late afternoon. Because my cousin obviously had her own woes, she almost never had the time to call. But on this particular day, surprisingly, she initiated a phone call – just wanting to talk. What are the chances? Here is what I recorded in my journal in this regard on the same day as the above entry:

Friday, December 30, 2005 – Unexpectedly, Cousin Kim called me today at about three o'clock in the afternoon. I was amazed to hear her voice because she almost never has time to call. It was odd that she should call me on this particular day because of what happened this morning at Mass. Her calling was just enough push to put me over the edge and share with her this morning's locution.

"Kim," I said. *"Do you have a blue ring that you like to wear?"* She promptly replied, *"Yes! I am wearing it right now."* Intrigued by my question, Kim continued, *"It's my most favorite ring – possibly more than my wedding ring because my husband Jim bought it for me when we first got married ten years ago. I wear it all the time. I love it!"* The next detail I knew was going to be the final test as to whether this conversation actually came from God or not. So I went for it and said, *"Kim, does your blue ring have a star in the middle?"* *"Yes, yes it does!"* she excitedly exclaimed. *"How did you know?"* she queried. Next, I shared with her all that had transpired at this morning's Mass and the prophecy that was meant for her and her alone. I assured her that she is on God's radar; he sees her and loves her very much. And how interesting, I mused with Kim, *"God used the imagery of the blue sea to get your attention – all your life, along with your father, both of you loved boating and the sea so very much!"*

About three weeks later, I boarded a flight to go and spend a long weekend with my cousin. The night before I left, when I was preparing my luggage, I was planning to give Kim an original handwritten copy of the locution, as well as a typed printed one. While I was preparing a sheet on the home printer, I received a word from the Lord. He said, *"Frame the words for Kim. Don't just hand them to her. Make it nice! Go to the discount store near the corner of Broadway and 8th Street. There you will find a blue frame. Place my words in a blue frame." "Wow, Lord,"* I thought. *"You really know how to make a gift presentation. Yes, of course! A blue frame would be the most excellent way to present your words about the blue ring."*

But to be honest, I did not even know that dollar stores stocked picture frames, let alone a blue one. It seemed to me that these places were known for inexpensive cans of cleanser, dish detergent, dollar bags of candy bars and the like. Besides, it was seven o'clock at night. Weren't downtown stores already closed? But I was not going to question the Lord further or argue with him. I knew that he infinitely knows better and so out the door and off I went. Sure enough, upon arriving, they were open, and checking in at the front cash register, the cashier pointed me to a section that actually had picture frames in it. Low and behold, among all the many wood and chrome frames stood one and one only blue picture frame!

Kim and I had a wonderful three day visit. She gratefully received her framed words and vowed to keep them next to a candle at a makeshift altar on her bedroom dresser. Over dinner one night, we celebrated the blessed assurance God was giving her. He was most definitely showering her with special graces. She then shared how, as a result of the cancer, she had become much more active in her church and was seeing the pastor there for spiritual direction. She even gave a reflection at a Good Friday service about a year before she passed on. Kim emailed me her manuscript and shared her thoughts with me. Recently, her husband Jim thought it would be good to pass her thoughts along to others in hopes of allowing Kim to speak to us from her vantage point in the afterlife. I am going to share parts of her Good Friday reflection now. May you find inspiration and solace in her words. Here in part is what she said . . .

"Friday, July 29, 2005 was the day my and Jim's world turned upside down, and in some ways, right-side up. We were at the doctor's office for a follow-up visit after some tests . . . The doctor came in, made small talk for a moment, and then Jim asked *'What is it, doctor?'* He said gently, *'Its lung cancer'.* To say we were shocked is an understatement . . . We left the office feeling shaken, lost, numb. During the drive home, we were silent for a while, lost in our thoughts. Then Jim said, *'Let's pray'.* My first prayers were very elementary---a simple *'Help me Lord, show me the way'.*

"Somehow we made it through the weekend. Monday brought more bad news. The cancer specialist said, *'You have a very advanced form of lung cancer -- it's not curable. At your stage, you can expect to live 6 to 9 months, without treatment . .*

.' Wow. There it was, the cold, hard facts . . . [But] my nine month anniversary is in two weeks. I'm still here. My bags are packed, but my flight has been delayed. What an opportunity, a new lease on life. In many ways I feel so much more alive than I did nine months ago. People who meet me just can't believe there's anything wrong.

"It hasn't been an easy journey. Without my faith, and the support and prayers of my husband, family and friends, I don't know how I would have coped with the many disappointments along the way. . . Through it all, I've never given up hope. Each disappointment was simply a test that we turned into an opportunity to seek new treatment options . . . After six new treatments, the latest scans indicated my cancer has stabilized, for the most part, for now. That doesn't mean I'm cured, but it does give me some extra time. What a blessing! Now, I'd like to take a moment to share with you what I have learned and the blessings that have come while on this journey. I learned a lot about myself. I learned that before cancer, I was sort of sleepwalking through life. I was caught up in the everyday hustle bustle, working hard Monday through Friday, and trying to squeeze in as much fun as possible on the weekends. We've always attended Mass on Sundays, but to be honest, I didn't do much during the week to really live my faith. Sadly, even morning and evening prayers had gone by the wayside. But what a wake-up call I received.

"I'm not sleepwalking anymore, I can tell you that! This journey with cancer has been a blessing in so many ways, a blessed tragedy as Father mentioned. I'm so much closer to my husband now, and to my mom and the rest of my family and friends. Cards, emails, Mass cards, books and phone calls have come not only from family, but even from strangers who care enough to comfort and sustain me. What a blessing to love and be loved! Most times, I can't wipe the smile from my face; I'm just so full of joy.

"Jim and I end each day as never before, in prayer. He so sweetly and fervently takes holy water from Lourdes and blesses my head, my lung, my liver, and prays for my healing. And I wake up each morning, watch the sunrise with such appreciation for his creation, and thank our Lord for another blessed day. I've learned so much about the power of prayer. After the cancer diagnosis, I felt lost and afraid. In my brokenness, I placed myself at the foot of the cross and prayed. I prayed as Jesus did; *"Father, please take this cup away from me, but your will be done."* What peace came to me from that prayer! I'm full of hope that the cup will be taken away, but I accept God's will without question.

"Early on, we called on Father Tobin for spiritual direction. At the time, I was still feeling a bit fearful of my terminal condition. I felt that I hadn't done enough good in my life, and I felt "unworthy" to meet God. Father explained that we're all "terminal", we're all going to die sooner or later, and none of us are worthy of God's mercy, but He gives it to us anyway. Father introduced us at Mass to the Ascension Community, and asked the community to pray for us. I really believe that day was a turning point for me. I felt so renewed in spirit after Mass, the fear completely disappeared. Today, I have absolutely no fear of the future, I know that God is with me, and live or die, I can't lose. Today I am healed; perhaps not physically, but definitely spiritually, and what a blessing that is. Is it any wonder that, for the first time in my life, I feel truly alive? Now, I certainly wish that I did not have this cancer, and could have received my wake-up call in some other way. But I'm so thankful that I've had the opportunity to change my life.

"None of us know what the future holds, and none of us knows the day or the hour that God will call us. Today could be the day for any one of us. I pray that if there's anyone here who feels like I did "BC", caught up in the hustle bustle, taking things for granted, sleep walking through life – that you'll wake up today and smell these beautiful roses that our Lord has given us. Give your husband or wife, mother or father and kids an extra hug today and every day. Take time to appreciate this gift of life and the glory of God that is so evident in His creation. And most of all, pray."

On Thursday, May 25, 2006, about one year before Kim passed on, the Lord spoke to me in a nighttime locution that he was going to take Kim home very soon. And in indeed he did. Cousin Kim died on Wednesday, May 30, 2007. What is most profound about this locution is that the Lord proceeded to tell me that Kim will have the ability to see and hear those who attend her funeral. He said, *"If you don't attend Kim's funeral, she will ask, 'Where's my cousin Gary at?'"*

Similarly, Maria Simma, in her vast experience with the souls in the afterlife once stated, *"A soul in Purgatory sees very clearly on the day of his funeral if we really pray for him, or if we have simply made an act of presence to show we were there. The poor souls say that tears are no good for them: only prayer! Often they complain that people go to a funeral without addressing a single prayer to God, while shedding many tears; this is useless!"* (*The Amazing Secret of the Souls in Purgatory*, Queenship Publishing Co., Goleta, California, 1997.)

Unfortunately, because of the thousands of miles distance, and the expense of air travel, I regret that I was unable to attend Kim's funeral, even though I knew she would be looking for me. However, Kim did appear to me in my bedroom one morning not long after her death. Here is how I recorded the event in my journal:

————————————

Friday, February 20, 2009, 7:30am – After reading from 5:45 to 6:30 in the morning the book, *The Peace of St. Francis*, something in particular spoke to me. It was the fact that St. Francis *"preferred duty to pleasure."* The point was stunning and caused me to rededicate my life to the Lord. Next, he interiorly spoke to me saying, *"fall back asleep, I would like to speak to you."* I was obedient and tried to do what he asked. But after thirty minutes had passed I was still wide awake and nothing. Then, suddenly as if overcome by a supernatural sedative, I fell into a suspended state and in walked my cousin Kim with another Kim, possibly the little girl my Uncle Ralph had adored and thus named his daughter after. They both looked thirty-something and extraordinarily beautiful.

Kim and I interacted for some time, about fifteen minutes. She was glowing with pure white skin and radiant golden-blonde hair. Given her propensity for style, she was wearing a fine-looking long white gown. In addition, my cousin was filled with lots of smiles, peace, joy, compassion and tenderness. Casually, she lay down on the sofa to talk. I remarked, *"Your skin is so white and pure. It's not the dark-skin tan we Italians and Latinos like to get!"* [This is an inside joke because Kim spent many a day tanning, either poolside at her Florida condo or on her sailboat in the Upper Keys. Anything that had to do with serene blue ocean waters, sunshine and sailing, Kim loved.] Next, my cousin joked back and said, *"No more lying in the sun and getting a tan for me!"* She was alluding to her new-found lifestyle in the afterlife.

We hugged and kissed many times in that momentous encounter. At first, I must say that she was hesitant to hug. Not because of not wanting to, but because she was pure spirit and without her body. I could tell she was not quite sure how these exchanges on earth played out in the afterlife. But then she took a moment, folded her hands and prayed to the Lord to see if it was okay. He said it was okay and she was completely relaxed about interacting the way we did when she was here. Next, we hugged and kissed some more. [We're an Italian family!]

Lastly, she held me very close to her, and sincerely and lovingly said she was very sorry for any wrong she had done in running our business venture in the 90s together – for hurting me in any way. I collapsed in her arms crying and said, *"No, no! Forgive me for hurting you and for being such a jerk!"* She laughed and said, *"No, you're not a jerk. The Lord loves you very much."* Because I was aware that she had direct interior communication with the Lord (more instantaneous than we experience here on earth), I asked her to beg Christ to forgive me for being such an idiot in this life. She tenderly laughed, loved and hugged me as I knelt at her feet crying with joy to see her again.

Eternal life and heaven is all about people that know how to forgive and want to forgive. Kim taught me that lesson loud and clear when she took the time to come and visit with me from the afterlife. Doing what she did, and saying what she said, taught me a powerful lesson about how we "work out our salvation" and how we get welcomed into paradise. We all know the ability to pardon is not rocket science, but nevertheless, it is very profound to know that it is at the heart and soul of the hereafter.

The prayer that Jesus taught us backs this up. He taught us to call God our Father and to pray . . . *"Our Father who art in heaven hallowed be thy name. Thy kingdom come, Thy will be done on earth as it is in heaven. Give us this day our daily bread and forgive us our trespasses as we forgive those who trespass against us . . ."* (Matthew 6:9-13)

Immediately after introducing the prayer to his followers, Jesus drew attention to its meaning when he said, *"For if you forgive others their trespasses, your heavenly Father will also forgive you; whereas if you do not forgive others their trespasses, neither will your Father forgive your trespasses."* (Matthew 6:14-15)

As I have said many times already, heaven is only for those who know how to forgive! It's not about how much money one gives to the church. It's not about receiving a scholarly theological education and getting ordained. And for most, it's never about doing the impossible – living a "perfect" morally squeaky clean life. Because of being human, God knows that over the course of a lifetime, eventually one is going to lie, cheat, look at another lustfully, experience casual sex – straight or gay, have extra marital affairs, "worship" homes, automobiles and other possessions and participate in other forms of idolatry. Unfortunately, for all of us, it's normal to do these things. And unfortunately, being normal along with leading a life of being judgmental of others; being unmerciful, vengeful, uncompassionate, ignoring the poor, unloving and unforgiving will, upon death, facilitate a one-way ticket to hell. And even more unfortunate, having what many believe to be a "faith" in God cannot save these types of individuals unless they repent of unloving behavior before their death.

If one is rich and therefore powerful (most people in this country are), living a life of no mercy, no compassion and no forgiveness is dangerous for the soul. So, as Dr. Phil likes to say, "Get real!" Let's get real with ourselves and embrace ourselves as the sinners we truly are. Then, let us go out and be merciful to others, spread our wealth around by caring about the poor, and start to forgive other people living all around us, ones who are steeped in their own sins and particular brands of brokenness.

Our Family's Conversation In Pictures

Mom and Dad, 1940 Engagement   Paula, in Her Wedding Dress

Christmas 1956, Family Shot

During WWII, Jim was in the Army, in France and Holland

Early 1950s, celebrating their second child

Me, Gem Beach, Lake Erie   Jimmy, Christmas 1959

Paula, Hosting a Dinner, Circa 1950s

Mom and Dad, 1960s Shot   Mom, Me and Jimmy 1966

Me, First Communion, Early 1960s

Mom and My Brother, 1972   Jimmy and Aunt Marie

1971, Family Thanksgiving Dinner

Mom and Grandma, Late 60s   Cousin Kim and Mom, Mid-70s

Cousin Kim and Husband Jim, Christmas 2005

Mom and Dad, Last Family Photo, Late 1990s

CHAPTER SEVEN

Jesus

My first encounter with Jesus was at the time of my near-death-experience. As I described in Chapter 2, he is pure love. In the NDE, when Jesus came down off of the luminous white cross, he embraced me as both Lord and lover. As I said earlier, visualize the best hugs you have ever had – possibly from a spouse, mother, father or friend. Multiply the hugs you are now imagining times millions and millions. You're touching upon a small sense of how much Jesus loves each of us. He wants to hold each of us and, like he did for my mother, say to each, *"I love you darling."*

Shortly after Christmas in December of 2005, while I slept in the nighttime and spilling over to the next morning, the Lord Jesus gifted a continuous conversation with me throughout the night. It was a lengthy dialogue where I remember saying to Him, *"You speak Lord and I will listen!"* Here is what I absorbed about who Jesus is, and what he would like us to know about himself, from that long night of conversation:

―――――――――――

Thursday, December 29, 2005 – Lord, Jesus, all of the Christian rites and Sacraments use humble elements such as water, bread, wine and oil. These poor elements point to the profound humility and the holiness of the very character of who

you are. When you came here Lord, through external signs –
those now famous symbols of humility; the manger, the bread,
the wine and the cross, you revealed to us your very nature –
love, mercy, compassion and forgiveness. Lord, you did not
show us yourself as high and mighty, but as a servant.

To this very day Lord, you continuously reveal yourself in
the unassuming flowing waters of Baptism, the simple broken
bread and crushed grapes of Communion and the pressed plain
oils of Confirmation and the Anointing of the Sick. Your humility,
Lord, and these humble elements of the Church Sacraments do
not make much logic to those, who, in their arrogance, crave
wealth, riches and power. The Sacraments of your Church, your
body, the Body of Christ make no sense to many. The noisy
excess of the world has disordered our passions and deafened
our souls to what is Real.

Many of your Father's children hunger for more of
everything, but they will never be satisfied until they find you. In
their arrogance, many try to flee death by acquiring more things,
working excessively, having shopping sprees, playing many
sports and other addictions – as if these pursuits could make
one eternal. However, pride, arrogance and earthly quests have
kept us from the humble knowledge of you in your Sacraments.
However, for the sick, the crushed, broken and the poor, their
humility allows them to readily welcome you, Lord. Their
emptiness and need are profoundly satisfied through the most
humble elements of the Sacraments. These modest
sacramental gifts are a stumbling block for those who see it all

as foolishness, but for those who are being saved, they are amazingly recognized by the humble, lost and broken souls who depend on the sacraments for eternal life.

———————————

I could never have written that on my own accord. That came by way of an intense and illuminating conversation with the Lord, continuing on and off, throughout an entire night of sleep. As a result, there is no doubt in my mind that he wishes to clear up misconceptions and underscore his true character of humility for us today. Let's face it; there are a lot of false notions going around about the nature of God. If you're like me, for decades I perceived God to be judging, condemning and ready to pounce on me when I lie, cheat or fulfill a lust, passion or desire. I had no idea that he is pure love and mercy, for those who are willing to humble themselves by believing in him and then going out and forgiving others. God is pure love and pure humility for those who are being saved. But, woe to the rich and the powerful who condemn, judge and control others – in their day-to-day sin, they fall under the judgment of God.

Also in this chapter, I believe Jesus wants us to know that he *is* unequivocally the Messiah, the Savior of the world. Why is that so important? Well, if you don't clearly know there is a guiding captain at the helm of a ship, how can you be assured that your boat, when in a storm, will arrive at its destination? Jesus *is* the Captain that we can count on to bring us all to heaven collectively and individually throughout life's tempests.

Until Jesus came on the scene, we humans were barbarians. We take for granted the order, and for the most part, the civility we have around us in the world today, 2,000 years after Christ and Christianity. Yes, a couple of World Wars and conflicts have marred the planet since his birth, but thanks be to God we're not living day-in and day-out with the meathead brutality of the early Egyptians, Greeks, Romans, Vikings, Aztecs, Mayans and American headhunters and so forth. When you or I go for a day picnic in the park, or to the beach and there are no brutal Vikings around or headhunters scalping us, we have Christ our Savior, the martyrs and the Body of Christ, both Catholic and Protestant, to thank for the civility of our world today.

Here is what the Lord conversed with me in this regard one night in January of 2006. Here is how I recorded it in my journal:

———————————

Sunday, January 1, 2006 – While I slept Lord Jesus, you came to me three times on and off throughout the night. You asked of me one thing – the same question three times. You inquired, *"Who do you say that I am?"* Each time I emphatically answered, *"You are the Christ, the Son of the living God."* After answering the question as I did, you replied back to me repeatedly, *"You could not know this unless it was revealed to you by the Holy Spirit."*

Lord, your coming on this occasion and in this way is reminiscent of the time that you arrived in the region of

Caesarea Philippi with the disciples. You had just been confronted by the religious leaders. They had asked for a sign, apparently to test and see for certain whether you were the Messiah. But Lord, you are no puppet and refused to give them a sign. Instead, without giving any further signs, a little while later you asked the disciples, *"Who do people say the Son of Man is?"* They replied, *"Some say, John the Baptist; others say Elijah; and still others, Jeremiah or one of the prophets."* Lord, then you said, *"But what about you? Who do you say I am?"* Simon Peter convincingly answered, *"You are the Christ, the Son of the living God."* (Matthew 16:13-16) Lord, you told Peter that he could not have known this unless it was revealed to him by the Father in heaven.

A lot of people wish to make Jesus out to be just some sort of a nice guy or a cute bearded prophet filled with nice sayings for wall plaques. For some reason, diminishing Jesus is an important agenda for some. Possibly those who do this may be just badly informed of the verifiable historicity of Christ as the Messiah, as well as the authenticity of the ancient scrolls making up Holy Scripture. Be that as it may, what makes Jesus the Savior of the world and different from Buddha and other great spiritual leaders, is the fact that Christ rose from the dead. We must always keep in mind that there is no grave with a body in it for this very real person in history. We have ancient graves for other greats, like the Pharos of Egypt for instance, but not for Jesus. He's an enormously larger than life figure and because of that fact, if he were just dead, there would be preserved to this very day a grave with a body in it for people to go and visit.

The fact of the matter is that Jesus is not dead. Three days after his burial he resurrected from the dead. That is a fact, not fantasy. Mary, Mary Magdalene and eleven other disciples saw him many times over. For forty days he made many appearances, even ate with his disciples and appeared to five-hundred others who knew him. No one else has ever done this. Why? Because no one else has ever risen from the dead, but Jesus did. Here is what I wrote in my journal in this regard:

Friday March 31, 2006 – In a late morning vision, right before awakening, I heard the voice of an angel speaking to me . . . "Consider this Jesus, is he God and born a man? You may say *'no, that's unbelievable!'* Was he humble? You may say *'no, that's unbelievable!'* But was he wise? You may say *'possibly.'* Did he suffer and die? You may say *'no, that's unbelievable!'* But did he rise from the dead? Yes! Truly this man is God!"

On Tuesday, December 19, 2000, the Lord Jesus came to me in morning hours, right before I awoke. He spoke to me about God the Father, the Son and the Holy Spirit and their very nature in this way, saying, *"God is great – to the enormous measure of his greatness, so too is his responsibility to his greatness."* That's powerful! Of course it is potent, that is God having a conversation with us – his words are Spirit and life.

That locution is one that I have shared with many over the years. It is significant and that is why I am sharing it again now. Think about it for a moment. Go to the countryside and gaze into the enormity of the night sky away from the urban lights. Focus in on the endless stars, galaxies, black void, planets and moon. Next, take a moment to reflect on the delicate intricacies of the human body; the mind, the heart, the veins, the toes, the eyes, seeing colors and how you walk or even swim and dance.

Here is what I believe the Lord is illuminating with the words, *"God is great – to the enormous measure of his greatness, so too is his responsibility to his greatness."* It is the fact that from the endless reaches of the heavens and the complexities of the human body to the unfathomable depths of the ocean – that all this greatness we see around us also tells an enormous "Love Story." To the same degree we see the vast grandeur around us, so too, that is exactly how magnificent and infinite God's loving responsibility is to the creation he has made.

What does that mean to you and me? It means God loves each and every one of us deeply. Don't let anyone say otherwise. *"For God so loved the world that he gave his only begotten son, that whosoever believes in him might not perish but have eternal life."* (John 3:16) God not only infinitely creates; he also infinitely loves and is responsible for his creation. The fact of the matter is that he, who created all things, was also willing to come to his creation and love it to death – even death on a cross. He is so amazingly responsible for what he has created that he was willing to suffer, die and forgive his persecutors – the very people he created. How awesome is that? If he is willing to do all that for you and me, should we not listen and join in the conversation, instead of acting as though he does not exist? Worse yet, not only denying him, some also use his name as some sort of derogatory expression or swear word.

If we are in awe of what we can see, just imagine how breathtaking everything is that is unseen. The Apostle Paul concurs when he writes, *"No eye has seen, no ear has heard, and no mind has imagined the things that God has prepared for those who love him."* (1 Corinthians 2:9) One night, in January of 2007, I was up praying at about three o'clock in the morning and briefly had an opportunity to share with the Lord, through his own initiative of course, some glimpses into what heaven might be like. Here is how I recorded the events of that night:

_____

Tuesday, January 9, 2007 – Lord, thank you for what Fr. J. [another Spiritual Director] refers to as "cooperative grace!" Lord, your grace is enough and amazingly you showered it upon me throughout this past night. I awoke at around three in the morning and was reading parts of the book *"My Life"* by St. Teresa of Avila. Then you inspired me to pray the rosary in a unique way. Using the *"Five Sorrowful Mysteries,"* I recounted the way of the cross and the death of Christ. Remorsefully, I also linked five personal failures that I wanted to confess to you and get off my chest. After each decade of the rosary, I sensed a growing lightness in both my body and spirit. As I sat up in bed praying and while I was still not quite finished – Lord, you walked into the room and gently asked, *"Can I take you?"* And of course I said, *"Yes!"*

Next, your great loving arms wrapped around me and you took me upwards through the top of the building. Lord, you are a great gentleman in the way that you came and gently asked to take me, lifting me high into the heavens. The peace and joy of being with you in the heavens is indescribable. It was my joy to yield completely to your will as I gave you great praise the entire time we were away. Lastly, you returned me to my bed. You placed me gently down and under the covers in the same tender way my mother or father did when I was a small child. It is my delight to be your little child, Lord! You left me to sleep for a while and then you visited again and took me a second time into the heavens. How enormous is the peace of your caress, the love of your embrace and the joy of soaring into the heights with you! Truly, eye has not seen and ear has not heard what you have prepared for us.

But Jesus, as he matured from childhood, was not on the "mountain tops" soaring into the heights with one foot in heaven, as one may think. He had work right here on earth to do. Although Jesus was God, keep in mind that he was also fully human. He lived, ate, drank, laughed, celebrated, had temptations, cried and suffered in the same way we do. Just because he was God, he was not exempt from being fully human too. He was like us in every way. From the moment he was born, he matured and grew in wisdom in the same fashion as any child today. His mother, Mary, and his guardian father, Joseph, had to raise him, show him how to tie on his sandals, the way to school in the morning and then help him with his Hebrew homework at night.

Jesus grew in the knowledge that he was also divine and that he would have to do his Father's will, suffer and die. This insight was not acquired the moment he was born. Over time, he grew in the knowledge that he, like Isaac, the son of Abraham was going to be sacrificed, killed for the sins of the people. However, he would not be treated the same way Isaac was, who was released at the very last moment from being sacrificed. Jesus had to go all the way.

On the surface, it seems farfetched that flesh needs to be sacrificed in order for life to be gained. It is not so mind-boggling if we think about the reality that sacrificing flesh is an every-day-of-the-week occurrence because most people consume meat at mealtimes. If it were not for the sacrifice of animals, life would not continue on the earth the way we know it now. So too, Jesus sacrificed himself, his flesh not as food for a day, but food for an eternity, feeding us forever within the realm of the spirit. In February of 2007, the Lord firsthand revealed further insights into this aspect of his life. This is what I recorded in my journal about the event:

Tuesday, February 20, 2007 – Lord, thank you for this morning's vision, where in it I was crying because you revealed to me a moving insight into your early adolescent years. In your twelfth year, while you were still yet a boy, it was at the Jewish feast of the Passover holidays that you began to realize that you were "different." You were just twelve years old when you grew in the understanding that you would be killed for your great love for us, your compassion and beliefs. You discovered, while reading the scrolls in the temple with the rabbis, that you would be sacrificed and killed just as the perfect young lamb was lead to slaughter at Passover time. You were so consumed by these inspirations that you forgot to board the caravan with your mother and father, Mary and Joseph, for the ride home. And because you are fully human, you came to these realizations gradually, through the power of reason and direct illumination from your Heavenly Father. It was here at this holiday Passover that you began to unite the symbols of bread and the wine and the festal lamb with your own passion and death that would come in about twenty years. A significant part of your suffering here on earth was connected to this twenty-year period where you had to internally wrestle with the knowledge that the inevitable was going to happen to you in your thirties. You knew that your death was going to be horrendous and humiliating.

Because of Jesus' death on the cross, we have an advocate, actually a "lawyer" who empathizes with us in every way. Jesus lived the life we live and thus he is adequately informed about our condition and he reliably pleads our case for mercy before God the Father. He is like the Old Testament high priest who had to intercede for the sins of Israel and offer temple sacrifices to God. However, Jesus offered himself as one final sacrifice once and for all. He can now plead each of our cases in heaven before God.

If this all sounds too farfetched, pick up a copy of the movie, *Defending Your Life* starring Albert Brooks and Meryl Streep. After seeing this romantic comedy about the afterlife, the idea of having an advocate in heaven will make somewhat more sense. In April of 2007, the Lord communicated the following to me about his heavenly "law firm" that has freely paid the price for you and me. That's good news. His services are free. Everyone can afford Jesus as their lawyer, especially the poor!

Saturday April 28, 2007 – Lord, thank you for the locution and gift of your communication in the night. In it you said, *"We have a high priest who is constantly pleading our case before the Father."* When we sin, Jesus, you are always speaking up for us before the Father. You are our advocate. Lord, you also said to me, *"We talk about you!"* meaning you, the Father and the Holy Spirit. Of course I was curious as to what you meant when you said that.

I suspect that as long as we are in the habit of extending mercy to others, even though we sin, you plead our case for leniency because you said, *'blessed are the merciful, they shall receive mercy.'* Lord, you showed me that when we do sin, you immediately have a conversation with the Father about extending mercy to us. It is reminiscent of Paul's letter to the Hebrews. *"Consequently he is able for all time to save those who draw near to God through him, since he always lives to make intercession for them."* (Hebrews 7:25)

So in the locution I asked you Jesus, what you and the Father talk about. You said, *"We don't talk about what you are doing wrong. We talk about what you are doing right! Mainly, how you show mercy and compassion to others, as the Father is showing mercy and compassion to you. That is the pleading I make for you on your behalf – what you are doing right."*

_____

That sure is amazing! The words of the Lord here go against everything many have ever assumed about him. Contrary to popular belief, God does not look at what we are doing wrong. He's looking at what we are doing right! How profound is that? However, when I don't do much right, there's a problem. That is why it is important to weave into our lives time to help the poor, the homeless, elderly, sick, dying, broken and lost. The more that we are doing things right, the more we are giving God the Father, Son and Holy Spirit something to talk about. Conversely, the more self-centered that we are, and as a result, do very little good for others, more-than-likely, it is then that we fall off God's radar. That's not a good situation to be in.

When I was growing up, the Smothers Brothers had a funny routine that they did quite frequently on their television comedy-hour. Inevitably, there was almost a weekly dig from Tommy Smothers to his brother Dick. Rubbing it in, Tommy would say, *"Yeah, well mom always did like you best!"* I think that sometimes Catholics and Protestants each like to think that they are liked best. Not to mention, among the Protestants, some Lutherans or Baptists may like to think they are liked best, over say, Presbyterians or Methodists. Catholic groups are funny too. Some like to think that God favors Dominicans over say, Franciscans. One day I was visiting a diocese-run church, when I happened to mention to the pastor that I was visiting from a Paulist parish. He joked, *"Oh the Paulists! Are they still Catholics?"* With that said, I was surprised to receive the following locution from Jesus in November of 2007. Here is what I heard him say:

Sunday November 11, 2007 – Lord, thank you for the locution in the early morning hours where you said, *"I see Catholics and Protestants as one people, one Church."*

It's nice to know that God's love and mercy is so great that he does not see division. He only sees unity. He is "color blind." His all encompassing love is reminiscent of those heroic moms and dads that have regular active children, then they go out and adopt disabled children and everyone gets treated the same. These are parents with huge hearts of love. After what I heard in the locution on November 11th, I can only now imagine that God has a huge heart of love for all his people here on earth. We're the ones with the problem of how to get along. For God, loving us equally has never apparently been a problem.

Whether Catholic or Protestant, one of the many things everyone agrees on is that Jesus will come again. Catholics in unison profess, at the time of the Eucharist, *"Christ has died, Christ is risen, Christ will come again"* All mainline Protestant denominations believe in the Second Coming as well. Jesus spoke of his return when he said, *"At that time, the sign of the Son of Man will appear in the sky, and all the nations of the earth will mourn. They will see the Son of Man coming on the clouds of the sky, with power and great glory."* (Matthew 24:30) In conclusion of this chapter about Jesus, here is a clip from my journal in regard to His coming:

––––––––––––––

Tuesday, June 24, 2009 – Lord, thank you for the locution in the night where you spoke, *"The sign of the Son of Man will be seen all over the earth."* Then you gave me a strong interior awareness that your "sign", the sign of the cross, will appear in the sky for many days so that everyone on the earth will see it and have an opportunity to turn to you. Yet, some hearts will be so hard and cold that they will deny the cross and its sign in the sky. Apparently, the sun and moon will be darkened for a time and the cross will illuminate the sky. Lord, you have said in the scriptures: *"And I, if I am lifted up from the earth, I will draw all men to Myself."* John 12:32

––––––––––––––

I suspect that when the sign of the cross appears in the sky, it will be one more example of God being merciful to us all. He'll be exhausting every last means to get our attention. When this event takes place, it will be like a *"Repentance for Dummies"* book. It will be a blaring sign, to non-believers and marginal Christians, to wake up and change. Here is how the Gospel of Matthew further describes this coming event.

"Immediately after the distress of those days, 'the sun will be darkened, and the moon will not give its light; the stars will fall from the sky, and the heavenly bodies will be shaken.' At that time the sign of the Son of Man will appear in the sky, and all the nations of the earth will mourn. They will see the Son of Man coming on the clouds of the sky, with power and great glory. And he will send his angels with a loud trumpet call, and they will gather his elect from the four winds, from one end of the heavens to the other." Matthew 24:29-31

There have been other revelations about the person of Jesus Christ. Following, are more entries about him from my journal. They are insights that were granted in the months right prior to this book's publication.

Sunday, May 9, 2010 – Lord, thank you for speaking this morning, saying, "[I] *bore in the crucifixion all of your diseases."* And so, Lord, interiorly, you have shown me that there is not a disease in any hospital room or doctor's office that you did not experience in your own brutal passion, suffering and death. When we think about the ravages and weakness of cancer, you experienced the same on Good Friday. You carried your cross in pure exhaustion, and then Simon had to help you. In the scourging at the pillar, you bore the pain of leprosy, cancer and all extreme skin disorders. At the crowing with thrones, you lived through debilitating migraines and brain disorders. All diseases, Lord, you experienced, and you have sympathy for all those who suffer today. All who are sick can turn to you because you understand. By your cross Lord, we are healed!

This was to fulfill what was spoken through the prophet Isaiah: "He took up our infirmities and carried our diseases." Matthew 8:17

Surely our grief's He Himself bore, and our sorrows He carried; yet we ourselves esteemed Him stricken, smitten of God, and afflicted. Isaiah 53:4

———————

The next revelation speaks to the age-old debate: Does Jesus save us by faith, by works or by both? It was at the heart of the Protestant Reformation controversy. Theologians, both Catholic and Protestant, often find it difficult to reconcile Paul's teaching of "faith only" and James, the brother of Jesus' teaching of "works."

———————

Saturday, Jul 10, 2010 – Lord, thank you for the vision this morning, where in it I saw a large circle. At the top of the circle [twelve o'clock], was printed the words, *"Salvation by Faith."* Then I heard you speak, saying: *"Walk around the circle, which are your works of mercy, compassion and kindness.*

Where does it bring you back to?" Then, Lord, you swiftly responded, *"It brings you back to 'Salvation by Faith.'"*

Lord, in this revelation, you showed that the circle is a life lived filled with mercy, compassion and forgiveness and it's your *complete* plan for our sanctification, but always leading us back to salvation by faith. It's a reminder and confirmation of similar lessons learned from the letter of James, *"You see that a person is justified by what he does and not by faith alone."* James 2:24

———————————

CHAPTER EIGHT

God the Father

It is impossible for me to write this book without taking time to share about the person of God the Father. One reason, is because it is he, whom I first met in my NDE experience. For those who were not raised with any catechism training, it is important to note here in this chapter that God is three Persons in one; God the Father, God the Son and God the Holy Spirit. Just remember this, one God – three persons!

But how is that possible? Nobody really has the answer to that because God is God. If God were other than God, then we would have the possibility of understanding this mystery. But because God is God, he is therefore infinite. Humans are not built to understand the infinite. We have a hard enough time understanding how to program a DVD player, let alone the infinite heights and depths of the nature of God.

With all that said, and having been momentarily on the other side, I think I can shed a small spec of light and some very limited insight into what is ultimately an unexplainable mystery of God in three Persons. Because the Bible tells us that we are made in the image and likeness of God, let's first look at our own humanity for clues of the trinity in all of us. As we do this, remember, from the earliest of ancient days, in the book of Genesis, God referred to himself as a plurality when he proclaimed, "Then God said, *'Let us make man in our own image and likeness.'*" (Genesis 1:26) If he was only one person he would have said, *"Let me make man in my own image and likeness."* But he did not. He said, *"Let us make man in our own image and likeness."*

We who are similar to God in our composition, are also made up of three parts; body, soul and spirit. There are three yous! That is why we have heard stories of certain saints who have experienced bilocation – being in two places at one time. Namely, in recent years, Padre Pio (+1968) had this gift.

Look at it this way. When you get into a car and drive down a highway, your body is physically in the automobile and it's operating the car skillfully – that is one part of you, your body at work. However, did you ever notice that while you are driving you can simultaneously speak with a passenger or take a phone call, safely we hope? That is your spirit at work, talking and recalling various memories and thoughts. Now, while you are having a conversation and driving, you also have the ability to experience emotions, regrets, joys and frustrations. That is your soul at work. The body and spirit sit inside of definition (words), while the soul sits outside of definition.

Words are completely unable to describe the very core, "soul" part of you. That is why we call some music, "soul music." That term means to say that although the music itself sits inside definition such as its notes and instrumentation (body and spirit), other wonderfully rich aspects of the music can not be explained or put down on paper. That unwritten feature refers to "soul music," and it is the musician's soul expressing itself outside of definition.

Did you ever notice the three parts of you can talk to each other? We call that, "wrestling with an idea," so-to-speak. When we wrestle with a decision or plans to be made, we use up all three parts to have a conversation about a particular concern. This internal chatter is a conversation going on inside of us every moment of our waking and even sleeping hours. Our dreams are a product of this triune conversation as well.

You see, if we were only one person, then we would be more like a computer than a human being. Computers deal with data in singularities, processing bits in orderly split moments of time. They do not have a soul or a spirit. They function and act in a single way and no matter how much data they hold, they are finite. Humans are much more advanced than this. We function in complete integrated conversations with ourselves to not only process data, but to also simultaneously consider many other complex factors such as good, evil, hate, concern, compassion, mercy, anger, frustration and love.

Humans, in a somewhat similar way are like God who is also three Persons. When Jesus was on this earth, he had a body like ours and he was fully human. He also had a Spirit, the Holy Spirit. Lastly, he had a soul – just as we do, but his soul was very God himself. When he was alive, like us, he was able to converse interiorly between his Body, Soul and Spirit. To this very day, this is how God communicates within himself. He is a community of three persons that talk creation out among the three of them. If God was a singularity, he would do things like a computer, cut and dry. But he is a community of three. He has the ability to balance the law, duty and the offense of evil with compassion, forgiveness, justice and kindness. Thanks be to God that God is a community of three Persons. If he were not, all of us would be in a lot of trouble because in that case, he would decide matters cut and dry like a computer – essentially throwing the book at us with no consideration for the good we do in this life. Thankfully, God can dialogue within himself and, as a result of that conversation, offer each one of us simultaneously perfect justice and mercy in a completely fair and balanced way.

A discussion about "God in Three Persons" is incomplete without drawing attention to Saint Augustine (+430) and his book, *On the Trinity* (De Trinitate). This original treatise turns out to be one of his most important accomplishments. According to Augustine, human beings are created in the image of God and therefore the mystery of the Trinity is imprinted in each one of us. Augustine started with God the Father as being Love. Saint John in his first letter tells us, *"God is love."* (1 John 4:8) But there is no such thing as love without a beloved which is why the Son is necessary. Ultimately, love can not just stay locked between two individuals or else it becomes sort of a dual egotism. The love between the Father and Son wants to be shared, which is where the Holy Spirit comes in. Therefore, God (Love), the Son (Beloved) and the Holy Spirit (Shared Love) proceed forth from them, being one God in three Persons. It is within this same triune model that humans are created, in order that we love and are not self-centered or egotistical creatures.

The previous chapter addressed who Jesus is in the mix of these three Persons. But in this chapter I would like to focus more on the person of God the Father. (The layout of the book does not include a further discussion about the Holy Spirit. We will save that for another time.)

One of the most comprehensive insights we have into the character of God the Father is Jesus' story of the "Prodigal Son." In the story, Jesus intends to give us an authoritative glimpse into the very nature of the Father. That's a good thing because many people are confused about him. They think God is a mean ogre just waiting for us to do something wrong so he can cast us all into hell fire. Jesus is going to clear up the misperception. Here is the story Jesus tells. It's worth knowing about if you have never read it. If you have, it's always good to read it again and again. It's that good.

Jesus said, "There was a man who had two sons. The younger one said to his father, *'Father, give me my share of the estate.'* So he divided his property between them. Not long after that, the younger son got together all he had, set off for a distant country and there squandered his wealth in wild living. After he had spent everything, there was a severe famine in that whole country, and he began to be in need. So he went and hired himself out to a citizen of that country, who sent him to his fields to feed pigs. He longed to fill his stomach with the pods that the pigs were eating, but no one gave him anything.

"When he came to his senses, he said, *'How many of my father's hired men have food to spare, and here I am starving to death! I will set out and go back to my father and say to him: Father, I have sinned against heaven and against you. I am no longer worthy to be called your son; make me like one of your hired men.'* So he got up and went to his father.

"But while he was still a long way off, his father saw him and was filled with compassion for him; he ran to his son, threw his arms around him and kissed him. The son said to him, *'Father, I have sinned against heaven and against you. I am no longer worthy to be called your son.'*

"But the father said to his servants, *'Quick! Bring the best robe and put it on him. Put a ring on his finger and sandals on his feet. Bring the fattened calf and kill it. Let's have a feast and celebrate. For this son of mine was dead and is alive again; he was lost and is found.'* So they began to celebrate.

"Meanwhile, the older son was in the field. When he came near the house, he heard music and dancing. So he called one of the servants and asked him what was going on. 'Your brother has come,' he replied, *'and your father has killed the fattened calf because he has him back safe and sound.'*

"The older brother became angry and refused to go in. So his father went out and pleaded with him. But he answered his father, *'Look! All these years I've been slaving for you and never disobeyed your orders. Yet you never gave me even a young goat so I could celebrate with my friends. But when this* son of yours who has squandered your property with prostitutes comes home, you kill the fattened calf for him!'

"'My son,' the father said, "you are always with me, and everything I have is yours. But we had to celebrate and be glad, because this brother of yours was dead and is alive again; he was lost and is found.'" Luke 15:11-32

Henri Nouwen in his book, *The Return of the Prodigal Son*, flip-flops the "central character" of the story, giving that vital title to the Father. At times he refers to Jesus' story as the *Prodigal's Father,* instead of calling it by the name which it is known, the *Prodigal Son*. I agree. Yes, it is true that the son musters up a lot of humility and good sense to come back to his father and apologize. That is difficult for most of us to do – to admit when we are wrong. So, in that regard, the son is quite central to the story. However, the merciful character of the father in this parable is truly heroic. Instead of reading his lazy-bum-of-a-son the riot act when he returns home, he compassionately welcomes him as some kind of war hero, not the loser that he actually is.

Perhaps many fathers that read this classic New Testament story would have a difficult time being merciful in this way, because many are all about duty and expectation and prone to little compassion. However, the father in the parable of the Prodigal Son shows us a completely different scenario. He is one of unconditional love and humble support.

In March of 2006, I was gifted a tremendous insight into the Father of Jesus' story. Indeed the following revelation about God the Father may have been given, in part, because of the contradictions and difficulties with my earthly father that I described in Chapter 4. Here is what I recorded in my journal about this event:

Tuesday, March 14, 2006 – In the early morning hours I awoke in tears of joy from a stirring and emotional vision. In it, I am standing on a dimly lit backstage waiting to go out and perform on a theater's main stage. The red velvet curtain is closed, hiding us from the audience. I and two other brothers are standing off-stage behind a black drape scrim and are receiving a pep talk from our director. He wants us to go out and give a stellar performance before a live audience. He admonishes, *"Go out there and cry, and make it good!"* In the show, we boys play the characters of three teenage brothers who terribly and suddenly lose their parents. As a result, we are each in desperate need of adoption or we will individually and collectively become homeless. We are about fourteen years old. While still offstage, the director huddles us together. He barks, *"Make this next scene powerful and convincing for the audience."* He's very demanding and continues saying, *"I want to hear heavy crying and sobbing. Got it?"* Although the pressure was on, we agreed and shook our heads saying, *"yes."*

Next, he pushes us even more. *"But please don't go out there and cry and let the audience believe that you are crying because you are all sad that your parents are dead. No!"* he said. *"These must be tears of joy. You must show tears of joy!"*

the director continued. And one last thing he said, *"Show the audience that quite unexpectedly, out of nowhere, a father stepped up to the plate, came forward and adopted all of you at one time. He rescued you from homelessness and kept your entire family together. Those are the tears of joy I want to see communicated."*

We came out of the huddle and he patted us on the shoulders. Immediately, we went out and positioned ourselves at front, center-stage to do the scene. The curtain opened, revealing a full-house. The theater lights went down and a spot came up on us three brothers clustered together. Barely holding each other up in emotional support, we wept heavily and convincingly many tears of joy. I remember feeling exhausted by the time the scene was over.

Next, wiping tears from my eyes, I left my brothers, walked down the riser steps at center stage and then sat upon one of them facing the audience. A spotlight followed me, the house lights came up and I could see the bewildered faces of the individual audience members. They looked stunned by our powerful performance. I began to speak to them, pointing out to the audience with my right hand and saying, *"Why did you come here tonight? Was it, to see a play? To see us brothers perform an imaginary story? No, my friends, this was not a play. What you saw here tonight was real life. We could have been angry and sad at the sudden loss of both of our parents. But our sadness has been turned to tears of joy, when just at the right time, out of nowhere, a father decided to adopt all of us. Did you come to see fiction? No, what you have seen here tonight is reality."*

Immediately I awoke wiping lots of wet tears from my eyes and face. I was still emotionally drained from the intensity of the adoption scene. In a daze, as I contemplated the meaning of all this, I asked the Lord to help me receive its interpretation. And of course he did. Without delay I was lead to the Bible passages that instruct us about our adoptions as sons and daughters of God the Father. He confirmed the vision with the Scriptures.

The first Scripture that came to mind underscoring our adoption by our merciful God the Father, is one that is frequently said as part of *Liturgy of the Hours* evening prayers:

"Praised be God and Father of our Lord Jesus Christ, who has bestowed on us in Christ every spiritual blessing in the heavens. God chose us in him before the world began to be holy and blameless in his sight. He predestined us to be his adopted sons through Jesus Christ; such was his will and pleasure, that all might praise the glorious favor he has bestowed on us in his beloved." (Ephesians 1:3-7)

This next scripture not only underscores our adoption as sons and daughters of God the Father but also the emotion of us crying because this is magnanimously so:

"But when the time had fully come, God sent forth his son, born of a woman, born under the law, to redeem those who were under the law, so that we might receive adoption as sons. And because you are sons, God has sent the Spirit of his son into our hearts, crying *'Abba Father.'* So, through God you are no longer a slave, but a son and if a son, then an heir." (Galatians 4:4-7) And lastly, one more Biblical confirmation of the vision's message:

"For all who are led by the Spirit of God are sons of God. You did not receive the spirit of slavery to fall back into fear, but you have received the Spirit of sonship. When we cry *'Abba Father'*, it is the Spirit himself bearing witness with our spirit that we are children of God; and if children, then heirs, heirs of God and fellow heirs with Christ, provided we suffer with him in order that we may be glorified with him." (Romans 8:12-17)

———————————

The theater stage story and its Biblical lesson taken in companionship with the story of the *Prodigal's Father* in the Gospel of Luke, speaks volumes to us about the very nature of God the Father. No matter how much of a sinner you are, no matter how much of a loser you are and no matter how badly your father treated you here on earth – you can have confidence that there is one Father in heaven that is all merciful and loving. He will take you back. He will forgive you. He will throw a party for you when you return to him, even right now as you are reading this book. You can confidently know that God the Father wants to adopt you and make you his very own son or daughter for an eternity. That's a long time! Like the prodigal son, all you have to do is fess up, return home, apologize to God for the wrongs you have done, acknowledge his fatherhood and he will take you back no matter what. What's the caveat?

When you kneel at your heavenly Father's feet and receive his mercy, he will then wish you to go out and be merciful and forgiving of all those around you. Mercy has to be a flow. It can't be a dam.

CHAPTER NINE

Mary & Joseph

As I mentioned earlier, in the chapter about Jesus, there are always those who wish to discredit him from his rightful title, "Savior of the World." Likewise, there are some, who for whatever reasons, wish to discredit Mary, the "Mother of God." Since about the time of the Reformation, there have been outspoken ones who want to deny her of our devotion and prayers of thanksgiving and adoration. Personally, I think there is something inherently wrong when anyone takes the time to put motherhood and a woman down, especially the Mother of God. If it were not for the motherhood of women, the whole cycle of life would be nonexistent. So too, without Mary the Mother of God, the whole cycle of Eternal Life would be nonexistent. Possibly, that is why Mary has many female devotees. Most women are mothers or have innate motherly abilities, and so therefore they get it. If more Catholic and Protestant men spent time connecting with Mary, more-than-likely there would be a plethora of more compassionate and merciful husbands, fathers and leaders in the world today.

What many fail to contemplate, or fully appreciate, is the fact that only after thousands of years of civilization and millions of women later, only *one* woman had a life worthy of being chosen as the Mother of God. Only *one* woman in all of history would ever have the resume and qualifications to do the job, to be the mother of God. What are the chances? Now if you or I went all our lives playing the lottery, then suddenly we won the jackpot, wouldn't you be excited about those phenomenal chances? Of course, and its doubtful anyone would play it down.

What did Mary actually do for us, if anything, that deserves our acclamations and adoration? A lot! When the entire world celebrates Christmas every year, we get the fairy tale version of her story. We see beautiful manger scenes for sale in the Christmas aisle at places like Kmart, twinkling stars atop city skyscrapers, halos on angels, glittering comet tales on Christmas cards and more. Combine it with sappy holiday tunes and it sounds like Mary really did not do much for us. She lived a fairytale! Mary appears more like a privileged queen in a romance novel, rather than the extraordinarily humble, longsuffering and obedient woman of God that she actually is.

Let's be real and put it all into a genuine perspective. Here is a woman that said *"yes"* to God. We should all take a lesson from Mary. Do not say *"yes"* to God or even like Isaiah, who once said, *"Here I am Lord, send me,"* unless you are ready for hardship, suffering and pain. Picture this, right after Mary said *"yes,"* her fiancé, unaware of her miracle pregnancy, thinks possibly she is a cheater more than a saint. How would you or I live with a horrible misunderstanding such as this and its corresponding interior suffering? Eight months into her pregnancy, Mary has the "privilege" to travel by donkey over hot, dirty, dusty roads and all of it so she can wind up in a barn lying on a stack of hay to have her baby. Not to mention the chickens and smelly barn animals prancing around. How many married women today, would say *"yes"* to that?

And the list of her heroic deeds for us goes on and on. Ultimately, she receives the "wonderful" opportunity to flee King Herod for Egypt, becomes an exile in a foreign country, has to learn a new language, and then barely escapes a blood bath of Roman soldiers killing hundreds of Innocents. Ultimately, Mary, wholeheartedly supports all her life what she thought was going to be a "winner son," but ultimately, is a loser by Roman standards, and witnesses his brutal crucifixion. And all those decades she lived day-to-day by Faith.

For more than thirty years, in fact, she lived within a very dark "cloud of unknowing," and she did it all for you and me!   In all reasonability, shouldn't this woman deserve some on-going love and devotion from all of us? If she had not freely chosen to say *"yes"* to God and choose to suffer these hardships, who then would have brought the world its Savior? No one! You and I would have been up the proverbial "creek without a paddle," perpetually drowning and forever lost. She was our only chance, and thanks be to God, she did it. She never thought of herself, she only thought about you and me, and that is why Mary toughed it out.

With that said, let me share an insight from my journal about Mary and Joseph. It confirms a little bit more about Mary being the Mother of God and also tells us some about the unique role that Joseph played in our salvation story:

Monday, February 13, 2006, 5:00am – I had a vision in the night. In it, the statues high above the altar of St. Peter's Church came alive. There were three statues over the altar and from left to right were Saint Joseph, Christ and Saint Peter. Suddenly, the statues morphed into the actual persons of Saint Joseph, the Lord and Saint Peter. The two saints turned left and right and entered into a conversation with Christ. Next, a voice, like that of an angel, came out of nowhere and spoke to me saying, *"Do you know how Mary is referred to as 'the Mother of God?'"* I responded, *"Yes."* The angel continued, *"In much the same way, from now on, I want you to refer to St. Joseph as 'the Hands of Christ.'"* I replied back, *"But why?"* *"Because,"* the angel said, *"When Jesus was a child he could not do things for himself. Joseph did everything for him. And so he is to be called 'the Hands of Christ.'"*

This vision sealed up in my mind that giving our love and thanksgiving to Mary for being the Mother of God, is the right thing to do. After all, the confirmation came directly from an angel. I figure we can trust angels because they, if anyone, should know what they are talking about. Also, the vision revealed the unique role Saint Joseph played in our salvation story and stimulated in me a great devotion to him. Particularly because working with the homeless, I was inspired to see Joseph now as *"the Hands of Christ."*

Joseph is a guy that serves the poor! How so? Well, Jesus was rich but he left his riches in heaven and became poor and "homeless." So now, there is this wonderful man Joseph, who has a willing heart to help Jesus in his poverty and his "homelessness." Jesus, in this life suffered both separation from his Heavenly Father and loss of his home in paradise. But Joseph adopts him and cares for him in his enormous poverty. How heroic is that? Joseph does for Jesus what God the Father does for all of us. He adopts us and Joseph adopted Jesus!

So, it was right after that vision I wrote this prayer to Saint Joseph. I will share it with you in hopes that you will pray it and ask for his help with all the poor and homeless in your community.

"Dear Saint Joseph, you took the poor Christ child into your home. For many years he could not do things for himself. As a carpenter and as a true laborer, you became the very hands of Christ. Help us to become the hands of Christ for those who are helpless, those who are homeless; for they can not do things for themselves as well. We build ourselves into a home to serve those who labor to exist through your intercession and in your son's Name, Jesus Christ the Lord. Saint Joseph, patron saint of the homeless, hear our prayer. Amen."

Another image of Mary that we all have is one of her standing tall, crushing the head of a serpent with her feet. This picture is for good reason. It is inspired by an ancient Biblical passage from the book of Genesis, as well as by a vision that the Apostle John had in the book of Revelation, which is recorded in chapter twelve. In January of 2008, I received a vision from the Lord backing up the same image and revelation. Here is what I recorded in my journal:

———————————

Saturday, January 5, 2008 – Lord, thank you for the vision this morning where in it, first I heard the words, *"Mary has shut the mouth of the serpent."* In the vision, I saw a serpent standing tall around a tree at the entrance of a garden gate. He could watch me and others enter, but we were not afraid of him or his "puffed up" terrifying presence there. He tried to look scary, but had no ability to sting with venom. He was disarmed and docile.

———————————

Obviously, the serpent is the devil himself. Genesis 3:15 says, *"I will put enmities between the serpent and the woman, and your [serpent] seed and her seed: She shall crush your head, and you shall lie in wait at her heel."* This is one of the most famous passages in Scripture because it is one of the first ancient mysterious prophecies in the Bible about a coming Savior. The Scripture speaks of future conflict between a Woman, her Seed, (Jesus) and the Serpent that deceived man in the Garden.

This same conflict is spoken of in other places as well— even outside of the Bible. There are many stories across multiple ancient cultures about a conflict between a woman, the child she gives birth to, and a snake or dragon. For instance, the story is even reflected in the constellations our ancestors projected onto the stars of the sky. The constellation Hercules is using its foot to crush the head of the constellation Draco, the Dragon. In mythology, Hercules had a divine father (Jupiter) and a human mother (Alcmene), making Hercules half mortal and half divine—a distorted presentation of the Incarnation. In some ancient accounts, the constellation Draco guards the golden apples (forbidden fruit) from Hercules. These apples had the unusual property that any mortal who picked them would die.

This is one example among many. Apparently, the original ancient story of the Hebrew Scriptures, initially written thousands of years ago, may have been passed around from culture to culture over hundreds of generations.

What does it all add up to? That just as by one woman (Eve) did sin and disobedience enter the world, so too, by one woman (Mary), righteousness and obedience entered the world. A woman not only initiated the first problems of the human race in collaboration with a consenting man (Adam), but a woman also initiated the salvation of the human race in collaboration with her Son, a fully consenting man (Jesus), who was bent on obediently following his Father's will.

The Blessed Mother has other kudos and images too. On my mother's birthday, Thursday, January 25, 2007, I received a locution right before waking. In it, I heard the words, *"Holy Mary, Mother of God, 'Consultant of Grace.'"* (As mentioned earlier, most locutions are rarely long or wordy.)   In this very short revelation, the word "Consultant" appears to be central to unraveling the sentence's meaning and lead us to an important spiritual message. According to the dictionary, to "consult" is a word that means to ask the advice or opinion of an expert, colleague or a friend perhaps. Professionally speaking, we all "consult" doctors.

The other key word here is "Grace." What is grace? There are two types of grace, "sanctifying" and "actual." Sanctifying grace lives in the soul beginning at Baptism and makes our soul holy. It is an unmerited act of God that gives us eternal life. Actual grace is transient and it does not live in the soul. It is a free gift from God, working on our soul from the outside to bring about some special good in our lives, for instance, when God gifts events or inspirations that help to solve a problem with a particular sin or resolve unforgiveness of a certain person in our life.

In the locution, *"Holy Mary, Mother of God, 'Consultant of Grace,'"* I take this to mean that Mary is *the* person for each of us to go to, who like a doctor, to ask for her advice about how to prepare ourselves to live holy lives and to receive special graces from God to make that happen. We can talk to Mary as we would any consultant and ask her for aid. Also, consultants are specialists with an expertise. Mary is an expert when it comes to grace. The Bible says that she was filled with grace (cf. Luke 1:28). When we go to her as our *"Consultant of Grace,"* she can accurately tell us what to do and can assist us too. In the words of the "Hail Mary" we pray, *"Hail Mary full of Grace."* Now, she has apparently also earned the title, *"Mary, Consultant of Grace."*

Sometimes visions have a spiritual meaning, but they are not readily known or seen. As it was with the Apostle John's vision in the book of Revelation, in instances like this, one may never completely know its interpretation. One such vision occurred in February of 2007. I will do my best to try to explain its practical interpretation out of the peculiar imagery that it contains. Here is what I wrote in my journal:

Monday, February 5, 2007 – In a vision this morning, I and a few others waited in a small house on an insignificant side street eagerly awaiting the birth of Christ. Everyone gathered was anxious for his coming. Finally, the word came by a courier that he was born. They sent me out of the house to go and find him. I walked up a side street and I saw Mary, Jesus' mother, in a beautiful neighborhood tree. Next, I saw Jesus. But instead of him being a baby, he was a full-grown man and covered in blood. I took him by the hand to go with me so that the others back at the house could meet him. However, as one could imagine, being just born he could not walk or talk very well. I helped him along. Once at the house he spoke, but surprisingly his words were childlike.

When I awoke, I prayed for the interpretation. Here is a possible explanation of the vision . . . Mary, who is the *"Consultant of Grace"* is the one who delivers Christ to each of one us to this very day. Her delivery of Christ into the world did not end at his birth. How do we know this? Well the Apostle Paul said, *"The gifts and the call of God are irrevocable."* (Romans 11:29) When God gave Mary the gift to be the bearer of the Christ, delivering him to the world, that was a forever gift.

Her role as womb and temple of the Incarnation has never changed. Through her, we find Jesus born anew in each one of us. And, although we are adults, we have trouble walking and talking since we are still babies in the Lord. Therefore, we are not to be surprised when many adults are infant-like in their walks in Christ. We should be patient with them. Mary is the mother of all those who continue to be the incarnation of Christ in the world today. Mary, through grace, gives birth to each one of us who are called by his name.

As I was writing this part of the chapter, I received a locution from the Lord where I heard, *"Bathed in a sweat of blood."* Apparently it is alluding to the fact that Jesus, the central character of this vision described above, was covered in blood. But it was not any blood; it was the blood of the Passion of Christ.   The Bible tells us this about his passion . . . *"And being in anguish, he prayed more earnestly, and his sweat was like drops of blood falling to the ground."* (Luke 22:44) We can be assured that all those Christians today who are the Incarnation of Christ, they being delivered to the earth through Mary will also suffer Jesus' Passion as well as the triumph of his Resurrection.

Before carrying the discussion about Mary further, I would like to share here a short clip from my journal taken from January of 2007 that substantiates this talk about Mary, her perpetual gifts, her permanent calling and the fact that the *"Call of God is irrevocable."* Here is what I wrote:

––––––––––––––

Sunday, January 28, 2007 – Lord, thank you for the locution and then a vision in the night. First, I heard the words, *"The call of God is irrevocable."* Next I saw the vision of an older professional who was seated and looking very contemplative. He was reflecting on once being called to religious life, got side-tracked in his career and is now being called again after a long occupation in business. He comes to the realization, once called, always called. *"The call of God is irrevocable!"* [God has been referred to as the *"Hound of Heaven."* Once called by him, one is forever called. He will track you down like he did Jonah.]

––––––––––––––

Through the most recent mystical appearances and revelations of the Blessed Mother at Lourdes, France – Fatima, Portugal – Medjugorje, Yugoslavia and Garabandal, Spain, it is evident that Mary is forever involved in the evolution of our modern world to this very day, right now in this digital age. Although, the latter two appearances of Mary are not yet officially recognized by the Church, they have a large following throughout the world. At Garabandal, Spain, in the 1960s, the Blessed Mother spoke of a soon coming Warning, a Great

Miracle and a Great Chastisement. At four o'clock in the morning, one Saturday in 2006, a mystical occurrence took place that highly backs Mary's various messages for our world today. Here is what I wrote:

Saturday, December 16, 2006, 4:00am – In a vision, an angel appeared to me and said, *"I must tell you two very important pieces of information."* I politely replied, *"Please do not share private information from the Lord with me."* But he insisted and sternly said; *"No!"* Then again he said, *"I must share it with you."* Courteous but persistent I responded, *"Please do not share this with me because then I will have to become personally responsible for whatever you tell me."* *"No!"* he replied. *"I must share it with you."*

What he said next caught me off guard. He said, *"Look, you're considered to be one of the Lord's 'saints' and for that reason I need to tell you the message. You need to know what's going on!"* Well, when I heard the "saint" word I became extremely uncomfortable with that inference and got a little edgy with him. *"I'm no saint believe-you-me. You have the wrong person. I am not a saint but a sinner and a loser!"* I retorted.

Angels can be pushy when they are on a mission. He ignored my resistance and had an agenda that he clearly was not going to compromise. Then he spoke these two pieces of information to me. He said, *"First, there are angels on the earth, at this very moment in time, that are agents of God's government and his eternal Kingdom. These angels appear* dressed as men and women and can intervene looking like "real" human beings at any time. Particularly, they are moving about at high levels in world governments to influence global affairs." He continued, "The angels can transform from spirit to human form and blend in while still retaining their supernatural powers."

He said he had one additional piece of information that I must know about. He spoke authoritatively, "Secondly, the Blessed Mother will also be appearing to people around the globe to influence the Lord's will in the world today."

CHAPTER TEN

Relatives and Friends

When I was a small child, usually on Sunday afternoons our family had a fairly regular ritual of visiting various relatives that lived in surrounding cities not too far from our home. Between my mother and father, the relatives were divided up into "two camps." There was one set of relatives on my father's side who were more middleclass and slightly affluent having nice houses and cars. They all lived near each other in nicely groomed suburbs. My father's family was a kindhearted people, very welcoming too and every time we visited we shared awesome mealtimes together. Then, on my mother's side, there was our poor Aunt Sarah, a humble woman that lived next door to my grandmother with her husband Peter in a small, very ordinary house on the railroad tracks of a tiny steel town. Freight trains blew their whistles while passing at full speed rattling the entire house at all hours of the night and day. The meals were plain and simple too. It was always spaghetti and *"ball-a'-meat"* as she called it in her English-Italian accent. The menu almost never changed.

It's hard to put into words as a child why, but it was Aunt Sarah's house that I mostly preferred to visit, not necessarily the other families with big nice houses, awesome dining and wealthy accoutrements. To me, there was something unexplainable about Aunt Sarah that was simple and *Real,* with a capital "R." Although poor, she was always smiling, joyful, compassionate and quiet, giving lots of hugs and kisses. We always got our cheeks pinched too! Standing only about four feet tall, Aunt Sarah was affectionately dubbed, "Aunt Shorty," and that always made her chuckle every time we said it. Because of the special bond I had with this humble soul, even as I got older, I always made it a point to visit her and Uncle Pete. She never judged anyone and always loved us just the way we are. I never recall her gossiping or saying a bad word about anyone, ever! She just didn't do that sort of thing, although that is a common practice in most families today as it was in ours. Surviving my uncle by about twenty years, in her latter days I visited Aunt Sarah in a nursing home. She died at the age of ninety-three in 2007.

About nine months after her death, one night Aunt Sarah suddenly appeared to me radiant with love, affection, smiles and joy. She was seated in a rocking chair gently moving back-and-forth and chuckling, as if I had just called her "Aunt Shorty" again. She was not ninety-something anymore. She was very youthful, looking about twenty-eight years old. When I described the appearance to Fr. F., he said her smiles and joy was a good thing, a solid inference that she is in heaven. Reflecting on this vision brought me to a well-known Scripture adding further affirmation and consolation about Aunt Sarah's whereabouts. [Jesus said] *"Blessed are the poor, theirs is the kingdom of heaven . . . Blessed are the pure in heart, for they will see God."* (Matthew 5:8)

All the while I was growing up, my mother had a wonderful best girlfriend by the name of Ida. My brother Jimmy liked her a lot too. At one time, I understand she had a husband and through that marriage had a brilliant son who eventually became a church pastor. But all the years that I knew her, she lived alone. She was one of those self-made 60s women, *"hear-me-roar"* types that had her very own and quite successful *John Hancock Insurance* business. She had the sharp ability to get right in there and talk with the men and could sell ice to Eskimos. Ida was a huge contrast to the naïve homemaker that mother was. Possibly because they were opposites, that was the attraction in the relationship. According to my mother's recollection, Ida passed away in 2000. I had not thought of Ida nor had seen her in decades. That was all about to change.

Early one day in September of 2009, overwhelmed by what I had seen and heard in an appearance of Ida in my room, I called up my mom at six in the morning alerting her to the fact that her friend needed our prayers. Here is what I wrote in my journal regarding that event:

———————————

Monday, September 28, 2009 – This morning, a poor soul from the dead came, a friend of my mom's. Her name is Ida. She had passed away about nine years ago. Today, she was a wandering soul, still drifting without an eternal home. How sad. The best way to describe her would be "homeless."

When she appeared, Ida was quite elderly and resembled how one might look right after death, very pale and sickly. I immediately recognized who she was, however.

My brother Jimmy was there too; peaceful and silently looking on as I grabbed Ida's hand to speak with her. *"Tell me how you've been since you died."* I said. *"They don't want me in heaven!"* she whispered; looking sad, worried and rejected. She continued, *"The angels said I am not welcome there unless I give my life to Jesus."* *"But, He is God!"* I emphatically replied. *"He is God, you must listen to Him!"* forcefully repeating myself. I then embraced her lovingly and said, *"Ida, promise me that you will do whatever they tell you to do when you return. You must promise me that you will do that."* As I continued admonishing here, I held her close and insisted she choose to follow the Lord. Thankfully, she agreed and then departed.

It seems as though, now that I am telling my story, more and more friends are willing to tell me theirs as well. A close friend by the name of Filomena, who is the chef in an area church parsonage, recently shared details with me from two unique encounters she had with the other side that are quite significant. After immigrating to the United States from Italy with her fiancé in the late 1950s, upon arrival they set out to get married and start a family in their new homeland. Within two years of the marriage, her husband was tragically killed in an automobile accident that also left Filomena in a coma for weeks. Their two little girls survived in the backseat, sustaining only scratches and other minor injuries. What happens next is remarkable.

After some weeks, Filomena came out of the coma and made progressively small steps in recovering her health. It was at this time that family and medical staff broke the news to her that her husband had died in the car crash. The information was overwhelming and as one could imagine, devastated the new bride and mom. As she tells the story in her English-Italian accent she said, *"I cried alone in my room every day for months-and-months-on-end, frequently calling out my husband's name."*

After months of uncontrollable sobbing, something phenomenal happened to help end the terrible sadness that filled her heart. Filomena continued, *"One night while I was asleep, my husband appeared to me and spoke in his broken English-Italian accent. He said, 'Filomena! What are you weeping about? Please stop your crying!" Every time you start to cry, I have to leave what I'm doing in heaven to come here and visit you. I'm happy where I am at. So please don't cry any more.'"* With that he disappeared and as Filomena tells the end of the story, *"It was all so real, he comforted me and I never cried again after that!"*

After a couple of years of gaining strength and taking physical therapy, Filomena had to go get a job and become the bread winner for the family, which she continues to do now, some four decades later. After a few years of being a hard working mom, she was comforted in her toils by a unique appearance of the Lord that changed her life. This is what she witnessed:

"One night while I was fast asleep, I was taken up in a dream or a vision to an old-fashioned Sears store near my house. It was a place that I frequently shopped for the children. When I got on the escalator, I looked up and I saw Jesus standing at the top waiting for me. As I got closer I said, *'I know who you are. You are Jesus!'* At the top, I stood in front of him and excitedly said, *'What would you like Jesus? I will buy you anything you want in the whole store. Anything! You just name it and I will buy it for you.'* Next, Jesus put his hands on each of my shoulders and said, *'Filomena, there is nothing that I want. Everything here is mine. What I want from you are your prayers.'* With that, he left me and I woke up immediately and in my bed thinking *'What happened to me? I just met Jesus!'*"

Another family's amazing encounter with the afterlife was recently shared with me by Catalina, who has been the organist and choir director for the same church in small-town America since the 1950s. Even at her senior age now, and after having given birth to more than a dozen children, she continues to serve and to play at services, sometimes five nights a week. Here is Catalina's family story:

"When my oldest son Marty was still a boy, my father was not doing well and was not expected to live much longer. My father loved his grandson Marty in a special way. Marty would hand him tools while they worked on special projects and car repairs. They always loved being together. One day around five o'clock in the morning, Marty heard some noises in the kitchen. Without waking the rest of the house, he went out to see what was going on. That is when he saw his grandfather in the kitchen and began to speak with him for some minutes, thinking he had come over to the house for a visit. Soon, my husband got up and went to the kitchen because he heard Marty talking. Just as he arrived, my father left by the back door of the house and walked out into the garden. Marty was standing at the back door waving goodbye to him. Marty told his dad, *'Grandpa was just here visiting us!'"* It was just about then that a knock came at the front window; Catalina received word from her sister that her father had passed away around five o'clock in the morning.

But sometimes, God kick-starts conversations among us souls that are living on earth right here and now, mainly so that we will help one another by extending healing hands of mercy, love and compassion. Recently, Mary Lou, shared a remarkable story about a time in her life, some years ago, when she was in the hospital and was scheduled for dangerous surgery. While still in her room, she remarked to her husband that it would be great to find a priest in order to receive the Sacrament of Reconciliation (Confession) one last time. Unfortunately, the staff did not know of a clergy member in the hospital and was unable to help. At the very same moment, Monsignor Biedermann, from Sacred Heart Parish, had just entered his car in the hospital's parking lot planning to return home. Upon opening the car door he heard an auditory locution, *"Someone needs to go to confession on the second floor."* Filled with charity and compassion for the sick and obedient to the voice of the Lord, he visited every room on the second floor asking if the person had called for a priest. Having no luck, he walked in the last room on the floor and saw Mary Lou. He inquired, *"Did you call for a priest? Would you like to go to confession?"* *"Yes!"* she replied. *"How did you know?"*

In many respects, the impetuous of charity seems to be at the heart of the dialogue God is having with us. He is moving everyone to greater selfless acts of kindness and love, modeling us after his son, Jesus Christ. One night, a visitor by the name of Alvaro had been staying at our house for a couple of weeks and was preparing to leave the next day to fly back to his hometown with his teenage daughter. I had only spoken to Alvaro one time, the first day he had arrived. Mainly, we spoke at length about his faith and interest in the things of God. He had a lot of wonderful insights and a lot of great questions too. Because this particular visit was the first time I had ever met him, I really did not know him or even what he may need while being this far away from home to make his stay more comfortable. The entire two weeks he and his daughter were very busy, mostly traveling the area visiting family and friends. We were out of touch, but that was about to change.

On this particular night, his last before having to depart for home, I walked into the house at nine o'clock at night and stopped in the bathroom on the way to my bedroom to wash up and call it a night. I heard Alvaro's voice in a far room talking and did not want to interrupt. While standing at the bathroom sink, the Lord approached and engaged me in the conversation of the night. Here is how I recorded that event in my journal:

Saturday, November 29, 2008 – On this night, I went into the bathroom, and while washing up, I heard an interior locution from the Lord while standing at the sink saying, *"Offer to take Alvaro the hour and a half trip to the airport tomorrow."* *"Be prepared,"* he continued, *"When you go, it will be a very early flight, so be ready to wake up at three in the morning!"* Then he said, *"Are you willing to sacrifice a little sleep to help him out?"* With an oh-so-slight hesitation, I said, *"Yes, Lord."* I walked out of the bathroom, found Alvaro and as prompted said: *"Hey Alvaro, do you need a ride to the airport?"*

He was stunned, as if I had been reading his mind. *"Did my sister call you?"* he said. *"No,"* I replied. *"How did you know?"* he inquired. Filled with frustration in his voice, he had just been on the phone for over an hour trying to find a ride. Gratefully he accepted my offer, but with a word of caution, *"Our flight is at six. We have to get up around three in the morning, are you up for it?"* Without hesitation I said, *"Yes!"*

At that moment, he was completely unaware of what prompted a strong positive response to such an early flight and ungodly hour of the morning. Not only were friends and family unable to help this poor guy out, the Airport Shuttle did not even want to take him either! The company did not resume operations until five, much too late for him to arrive in time for a six o'clock flight. To make matters worse, the ride that he had counted upon cancelled at the twelfth hour, leaving no opportunity to make alternate plans. He was at that very moment out of options and out of luck. But God had mercy upon Alvaro and used a poor loser like me to extend help to someone in need.

_____

Well, there is not enough room here in this book to tell all the many stories that I am now aware of since I have begun to tell mine. But to me, it is evident that the conversation is going on all around us, both here and in the afterlife. Specifically, in this chapter it was important to share a few stories from others and including others because it illustrates that God is working in all of our lives continuing his dialogue with us. We only have to believe in him, trust him, pray and follow him in a life of sharing mercy, compassion and forgiveness.

CHAPTER ELEVEN

The Poor, Homeless, Lost And Broken

Unbelievably, God daily suffers rejection by the many who see his handiwork in nature, yet all the while ignore him and pretend as though he doesn't exist. When God physically came to the earth, he was also despised and rejected, primarily by the rich and powerful. This is one reason why, to this very day, God is mystically present in the poor, broken, despised and rejected living among us. God is no stranger to the rejection and suffering of the poor, and therefore he lives in solidarity with them.

Dorothy Day (+1980), the founder of the Catholic Worker movement and advocate for the poor once said, *"Christ remains with us not only through the Mass but in the 'distressing disguise' of the poor. To live with the poor is a contemplative vocation, for it is to live in the constant presence of Jesus."* Mother Teresa of Calcutta once said, *"At the end of life we will not be judged by how many diplomas we have received, how much money we have made,* [or] *how many great things we have done.* [Because Jesus said,] *We will be judged by – 'I was hungry and you gave me to eat. I was naked and you clothed me. I was homeless and you took me in.'"*

Saint Faustina Kowolska in the mid 1900s concurred with this notion when she recorded an amazing encounter with God himself in her journal. One day, St. Faustina encountered a poor beggar of a young man at the front gate of the convent. She had been placed in charge of serving the homeless that occasionally would show up pleading for help. In her own words, she tells the story this way . . .

_____

"There was this young man, emaciated, barefoot and bareheaded, and with clothes in tatters, was frozen because the day was cold and rainy. He asked for something hot to eat. So I went to the kitchen and found nothing there for the poor man. But, after searching around for some time, I succeeded in finding some soup, which I reheated, and into which I crumbled some bread, and I gave it to the poor young man, who ate it. As I took the bowl away from him, he [suddenly] gave me to know that he was the Lord of heaven and earth. When I saw Him as He was, He vanished from my sight. When I went back in and reflected on what had happened at the gate, I heard these words in my soul: *'My daughter, the blessings of the poor who bless Me as they leave the gate have reached My ears. And your compassion, within the bounds of obedience, has pleased Me, and this is why I came down from My throne – to taste the fruits of your mercy."* Diary of Maria Faustina Kowalska,* Notebook IV, #1312.

_____

In the Bible, Jesus also tells us a story about the "Rich Man and Lazarus" which is significant in this same regard. As you read the story below, keep in mind that the real sin of the rich man is not prostitution, it is not for being adulterous-straight or promiscuous-gay and it is not for lying, cheating or stealing either. The real sin of the rich man that winds him up in hell is what he actually had complete control over; he was arrogant and unmerciful to the poor and presumably others. He was so haughty; he could not even see the utter poverty of Lazarus. Further, because of his uncompassionate behavior here on earth, when he asks for mercy in the afterlife, mercy is denied him. Anyone that has hopes of going to heaven, there is an important lesson to be acknowledged here. This is only one of many significant things Jesus says and does that backs up his claim that God desires "mercy, not sacrifice." If you have never read the story, please enjoy its intricacies. If you know the story, read it slowly again and pray for the Holy Spirit to enlighten you as you entertain its various levels of meaning.

[Jesus said,] "There was a rich man who was dressed in purple and fine linen and lived in luxury every day. At his gate was laid a beggar named Lazarus, covered with sores and longing to eat what fell from the rich man's table. Even the dogs came and licked his sores.

"The time came when the beggar died and the angels carried him to Abraham's side. The rich man also died and was buried. In hell, where he was in torment, he looked up and saw Abraham far away, with Lazarus by his side. So he called to him, *'Father Abraham, have pity on me and send Lazarus to dip the tip of his finger in water and cool my tongue, because I am in agony in this fire.'*

"But Abraham replied, *'Son, remember that in your lifetime you received your good things, while Lazarus received bad things, but now he is comforted here and you are in agony. And besides all this, between us and you a great chasm has been fixed, so that those who want to go from here to you cannot, nor can anyone cross over from there to us.'*

"He answered, *'Then I beg you, father, send Lazarus to my father's house, for I have five brothers. Let him warn them, so that they will not also come to this place of torment.'* Abraham replied, *'They have Moses and the Prophets; let them listen to them.'* *'No, father Abraham,'* he said, *'but if someone from the dead goes to them, they will repent.'* He said to him, *'If they do not listen to Moses and the Prophets, they will not be convinced even if someone rises from the dead.'"* Luke 16:19-31

Jean Vanier, the founder of l'Arche communities for the disabled, whom I spoke of earlier in this book, expands upon the lessons to be learned from "Lazarus and the Rich Man." While speaking on radio with Lydia Talbot, he once said, *"I think there is a whole mystery which we find in Luke. Lazarus was an excluded outcast, a leper, and he is the one that enters into the kingdom. The rich man, who wasn't able to see him, rejected him. He goes into the place of torment. You see, the danger for rich people is that they become frightened and they build up barriers around their hearts, defense mechanisms, because they have to preserve their riches, preserve their image, preserve their power. So they become people of with lots of fear, whereas Lazarus has nothing to defend. He's just himself."*

In September of 2009, a poor homeless soul from Purgatory appeared to me, quite possibly someone who knew me from the streets or whom I may have served under the bridges. Now having read the story of the "Rich Man and Lazarus," one can't but help to feel for the poor soul described here, especially because of the wretched condition he was in. Here is what I recorded about the encounter in my journal:

Monday, September 28, 2009 – One recent morning, a young man about thirty-something appeared to me. At first I thought he might be a demon because he was in such bad shape and even scary-looking condition. So I poured Holy Water on him, just to be sure he wasn't the enemy! He responded humorously to the drenching and said, *"Yuk! "Why did you do that to me?"* I then realized he was a poor soul from the afterlife, but he was inept and confused. That prompted me to ask, *"When did you die?" "A half hour ago"* he replied. He was definitely a newbie to the afterlife. Apparently, from his tattered looks, he was a homeless person – one in jeans, basic t-shirt and his teeth were in bad need of repair. At the time of his taking leave from my room, I reassured him that my Mass intentions would be offered for him the next day, praying that the Lord would grant him eternal rest.

Some people believe that Jesus said, *"The poor you will always have with you,"* because he was encouraging us to realize this will always be an unmanageable plight and because it is so large, so-as-if-to-say, *"Ignore the problem as you wish."* Wrong answer! Jesus said, *"The poor you will always have with you,"* in part, because without the poor the middle-class and the wealthy do not have the ability to *"lay up treasures in heaven."* We need the poor, they will always be with us, because by seeing them, they help us middle-class-rich people to go to heaven. They give us the chance to practice the virtues of charity that make heaven possible. If we did not have the poor, the middle-class-rich and the ultra wealthy folks too, would remain self-centered and thereby doomed to the fate of the rich man in Jesus' story.

In the summer of 2008, I was, for one week, visiting a homeless ministry when the director got in my car while hitching a ride back to his home a few miles away. Candidly he said, *"I disagree with guys like you coming here and handing out rosaries to homeless people. I wish you wouldn't have done that today,"* I remained silent. He continued, *"Now I have to deal with the Rescue Mission across the street seeing our homeless people over there with rosaries hanging around their necks. They're Protestants and they don't want to see Catholic rosaries paraded around and irreverently draped over peoples' heads."* He escalated the discourse further by holding the rosary hanging in my car and said, *"And furthermore, I don't like it when people hang rosaries around their necks or from the rearview mirror of a car, its disrespectful!"* Of course, I strove to understand this odd point of view and continued to remain silent, never discussing his sore subject again.

Not long before this man's angry encounter, the Blessed Mother had granted me an auditory locution of her voice on Saturday, April 26, 2008. I had awoken in the middle of the night, after a horrific attack of the devil in a vision. To counter the assault, I sat up in bed and prayed the rosary at four o'clock in the morning. While praying, a beautiful woman's voice, made of pure crystal and total charm, spoke out of nowhere, saturating the entire room with sweetness, *"I will help you!"* she said. The amazing audio of her voice was better than anything that can be heard in an ultramodern movie theater's surround sound system. Drenching every fabric of the space with her charismatic presence, peace and consolation, I overwhelmingly knew the Blessed Mother had just spoken to me. Wow! From that night forward, after hearing Mother Mary say, *"I will help you!"* I was encouraged to never worry about any type of difficulties again. That was good enough for me. Since Mary is going to help me, there is really nothing ever to be concerned about, even if someone might get angry because I was passing out Mary's rosaries to the homeless and cheering on devotion and prayers to her! But I digress and I am actually sharing this story for another reason.

In July of 2008, not long after the encouraging words from the Blessed Mother, the conversation about the rosaries was ready to escalate and heat up even more. Here is what I recorded:

Thursday, July 17, 2008, 7:00am – In the early hours of the morning, I received a vision that our newly formed congregation to serve the homeless, *Servants of the Father of Mercy,* had received its first piece of mail at a new post office box established just about a week ago. In the early morning revelation, I saw my hand enter the box and surprisingly, I pulled out our first-ever piece of mail. [At this juncture in time, we were brand-spanking-new, no one had even heard of our name or address, but a few very close friends.] While in the neighborhood of the post office, I stopped in to check the mail and to see if the vision had any validity to it. Miraculously, there was one piece of mail laying there inside the box, just as I saw it in the revelation. I thought to myself, *"Who knows our address and that we even exist? This is really strange!"* The post card was actually a notice to pick up a small package at the counter. Upon opening it, the box was filled with handmade rosaries intended for us to give out to the homeless and donated by someone whom I had never heard of, or met before, according to the return address. There was no note inside. So, it was not a donation of money that first arrived for our newly formed nonprofit, it was a gift directly from the Blessed Mother!

A couple of weeks after this, I had the inspiration to investigate the return address and find the person behind the miracle rosaries. The donor was an elderly woman in her eighties, who spends most of her time at home, whiling away the hours making them for missionaries. She told me on the phone, *"When I read in an old newspaper, or magazine recently, that you gave rosaries to the homeless, I made them extra long so they can be placed over their heads."* I responded, *"Maam, it would have been impossible for you to have read about us or our address in any publication, we're brand new, no one has ever heard of us!"* She never did find the journal that she thought she saw the organization listed in.

The first miracle taking place here was the early morning vision that later that same day brought me to the post office and "got the ball going." The second is the fact that the donor apparently saw a vision too; one containing our ministry's name and address inside of a journal article that does not really exist. The third miracle is that rosary maker, by the power of the Holy Spirit, was inspired to make the rosaries long enough to fit over the head of a homeless person, countering what had happened a few weeks earlier by the man in my car. Lastly, the name of the woman is a miracle too – Claire Donner. Her name, when translated from the French, Claire meaning *"clear"* and Donner meaning *"to give."* Her name loosely translated means *"Clear Giver."* Only God could orchestrate a miracle with this many intricacies and layers to it.

These extraordinary events in this chapter shored up for me the fact that God is primarily concerned about the poor, the homeless, the sick and the dying. Since he is so concerned, we should be too and go and do the same.

CHAPTER TWELVE

Lessons Learned

Chapter one began with the telling of my near death experience. In particular, there is a lesson to be learned in the account of passing through the total blackness. The experience of going through the darkness is frequently sited and shared by others who have had a NDE experience. Apparently, the "black tunnel" is a sign and a symbol of our earthly need for faith in dark times. When I was in the blackness of death, it was my faith in God, fostered here on earth in dark times, which facilitated my rescue and brought me into the light.

However, a person does not need to have a NDE to pass through the darkness and experience a test of faith. In this lifetime, all the dark moments we experience are tests of the ultimate blackout each will have at the time of death. Cultivating faith right here and now, while we are still on earth, gets us ready for the big-one, so-to-speak. Intuitively, we all know that we should have faith in dark times, such as when we have lost a job, experienced a terrible accident, a divorce, loss of a child, etc. But do we realize how important it really is to have faith in all the dark times of our lives?

Right after my near death experience, a good friend, Scott who is of the Jewish faith, shared his own experience of passing through the darkness and meeting God on the other side. Here is how I recorded his story in my journal right after hearing it.

_____

Wednesday, October 26, 2005 – I met with my friend Scott today at Literati Café. He also had a God-encounter in 2000, while on a bicycling trip in the Desert Southwest with a friend. He had biked into a tunnel, alone. Once in the middle, unexpectedly, he was plunged into total blackness and could not see either end. The fear was tremendous as he groped the walls, passing slowly, step-by-step, and struggling with every fabric of his being, as he trusted God and had Faith that he would make it to the other side. That evening at the campsite, suddenly God descended from heaven, overshadowing Scott with his presence, shortly after midnight, while he was sitting on a hilltop high above the camp ground looking at the peaceful starlight of the pitch black sky. God chose to console Scott and reveal himself to him right after he had passed the test of the enormous faith-encounter in the black tunnel. Although not having a NDE, Scott experienced the black tunnel that many speak of, literally!

Scott and I also spoke about how when God reveals himself to us in the darkness, by our own free will, the response must be to choose God, more than ever going forward. If we should turn our backs on God after such a revelation, we would not do so in innocence as we did at other times in our lives when God seemed elusive. If we turn our backs now and do not choose to follow him it would be out of gross error and eternal damage to the soul. *"To whom much is given much is required."* (cf. Luke 12:48)

———————————

As in the "Rich Man and Lazarus," Jesus' parable shared earlier; similarly this book also contains lessons learned from my family's own story in the hereafter. In part, like Jesus' parable, it is a story about a man speaking back to us from the afterlife, namely my father. I sense that he and my mother are encouraging me, since their passing, to share our family's lessons learned. There's no doubt that my father is proud of what I am doing in this book. Particularly because it proclaims the message of God's mercy and forgiveness that he is a beneficiary of, from his unique vantage point in the afterlife. In part, my dad is accomplishing in this book what the rich man had hoped to do through Abraham, but was not done because he did not deserve mercy or any special consideration.

Putting it all into perspective, my father suffered greatly in Purgatory; however, by speaking from the afterlife here, he does not wish anyone reading this to have to undergo much of the same. It is better to learn one's lessons of mercy, compassion, kindness and forgiveness in this life, than to have those issues purged out in the hereafter. At least on earth, if one needs a break from the pressure of thinking through love and charity – there is always the possibility of a cleansing walk, inspiration at the movies, or having a comforting piece of chocolate cake. In Purgatory, there are no consolations. For many it can be isolation, desolation and suffering and with no breaks. One should always remember, heaven is a place only for those who know how to forgive, and it's better to work that out sooner than later.

This book speaks a lot about being merciful to others, since our going to heaven basically hinges on Faith in God *and* heroic acts of compassion to those around us. But what is mercy? Jesus said, *"Blessed are the merciful, they shall obtain mercy."* (Matthew 5:7) Succinctly, mercy is *not* giving to others what they deserve, but giving them the opposite. That is hard to do, isn't it? It can be illustrated this way . . .

A few months ago I stopped in at a breakfast diner and sat at a fairly empty counter on one of the barstools. There was no initial conversation with the server but, *"Coffee please. Give me a minute to read the menu,"* – you know, the usual restaurant ordering chit chats. After dropping off the coffee, the young lady occasionally passed by, but twenty-five minutes later still had not stopped by with refills or had taken the order. Once I realized, that for whatever reason, I was not going to be served; I paid the coffee at the front register and left the server a five dollar tip.

Once in the car, I thought about what had just happened. The usual way to respond to this sort of unkindness is to call it to the attention of the server, possibly have a few words or report the incident to the manager or owner. All of which probably is what the person may have "deserved." But mercy is about giving the person the opposite of what they deserve. In this instance, I thought to myself, *"What is the opposite here? I* know! *The opposite would be to give an awesome tip as if I had just experienced winning customer service."* So, that is exactly what I did. That was mercy in action. In hindsight, I suspect that the person learned more from receiving mercy than could have been learned by the usual reprimanding methods. She will forget ninety-nine percent of her customer encounters; this particular encounter will never be forgotten. It will always speak to her heart, calling her to conversion. That's what mercy does; it calls each one of us to change.

Adults and children both need mercy in order to grow in the knowledge of a loving God, but children need huge amounts of it in special ways. How does our definition of mercy play out with little ones? Similarly, as it did in the story about the server. Fathers and mothers are God's loving representatives here on earth. Little ones learn about the characteristics and qualities of God through their parents' merciful or unmerciful behavior. As we all know, sometimes children mess up really bad and they may deserve a severe scolding, but "the law of mercy" tells us to make it lighter or completely opposite of what is expected. For instance, the next time a child gets a "D" or "C" in say, math or science on their end-of-year report card (all the while dreading to come home), try surprising the little one with, *"Don't worry, we'll work on that harder next year. Let's go out and have a nice big dish of ice cream and celebrate the beginning of summer break!"* Over time, children will succeed and grow more from mercy than the traditional and confrontational ways of handling these sorts of things. Facilitating change in children, as it is in adults, is always a delicate balance of the law, discipline, repentance and more than anything else, lots of genuine mercy.

Frequently, many recognize that they want to be understanding and forgiving, but don't know if they have completely achieved the goal. In this regard, we've heard it said, or have even said it ourselves; *"I forgive, I just haven't forgotten."* That dilemma raises the question, *"How do I know that I have sincerely forgiven someone?"* There are two ways that I am aware of, that one can be certain.

First, the measure you are merciful and forgiving of yourself, that is itself a strong indicator of how merciful you are toward others. That's powerful to think about! Only you and I know best the same sins, failures and errors that are being committed time after time throughout the span of our own lives. Interiorly, the more that one can have a compassionate internal conversation about these errors saying something like, *"That's okay, with God's help, I'll do better next time."* Or, *"Jesus, I trust in you to change this in my life."* The more that one's interior dialogue toward self is patient and kind, it is also a strong indication others will be treated with the same love and understanding. However, the more that the interior self-dialogue is condemning and unkind with phrases like, *"You idiot, you did it again!"* Or becoming despondent saying, *"You can keep working harder at this but you will never conquer it."* Obviously, one clearly has the same ability to be judgmental, impatient and condemning of others. Therefore, the best place to begin living a life of mercy and forgiveness is right within one's self.

Presumably, it is unlikely that God will ever perfect a soul here on earth from habits or patterns of sin, if the person entertains even the slightest judgmental or unkind attitudes in his or her heart and mind toward others. God allows each of us to remain in repetitive sins because it is his way of keeping us humble, dependent on receiving his mercy and thus we are obligated to be merciful toward others.

Look at it this way; when one harbors even the slightest judgmental attitude toward others (almost all of us do); it's not in God's best interest to provide perfection to anyone living with that mindset. Why? You and I both know that the more perfect one becomes, more often than not, a bad attitude comes along with it; being impatient, unkind and unforgiving. We say phrases to ourselves and others like, *"Why doesn't he get it?"* or *"She's so stupid!"* and worse yet, *"I would never do what he just did. How rude is that?"* In our "perfectness" and our self-righteousness, we angrily walk away from another's brokenness, judging them and condemning them. In love with our own perfection, we go out and belittle others by spreading hate, discord, lies, exaggerations and disharmony. Why would God want to grant perfection to anyone that he knows is going to go out and beat up the little guy in his brokenness? He won't. Here lies the reason why any person with hopes of obtaining heavenly help to become truly perfect, by God's standards, must also pray for and pursue the complete virtues of charity, patience, kindness, meekness, gentleness, empathy and sympathy for others. It is within the context of a hundred-percent-of-the-time nonjudgmental attitude, that God grants complete, personal sanctity to each of his children. How many people do you know that are willing to live that way?

Bede Jarrett, a pastor from England, before the time of his death in 1934, gave a similar explanation as to why we are not perfected here on earth and the reason most will remain with continuous imperfections of sin until they are buried six-feet-under. He said, *"If we were truly humble, we should never be astonished to find ourselves giving way to sin. We should indeed be horrified but not surprised . . . Once we have really begun to try to see what we are like, we recognize ourselves to be the most evil of creatures. This is no mock humility, for there is no room for anything mock in the spiritual life. This is true humility . . . God wishes me out of my past sin to come nearer to him, to find somewhere in that unhappy past a motive too for love."*

While basking in God's kindness and forgiveness of my own sin, that self-sinful realization should indeed propel me to genuinely love others who are broken and sinful as well – not condemn them. Yet, some will read this and be completely oblivious to their sins. If one feels perfect, better than others or has a sense of being right (self-righteous) all the time – that is in itself a false notion and a deception of the largest kind.

Jesus tells a parable about a similar lesson. The story is titled, "The Unmerciful Servant" Here it is, check it out:

"Then Peter came to Jesus and asked, *'Lord, how many times shall I forgive my brother when he sins against me?* Up to seven times?' Jesus answered, *'I tell you, not seven times, but seventy-seven times.'* Therefore, the kingdom of heaven is like a king who wanted to settle accounts with his servants. As he began the settlement, a man who owed him ten thousand talents was brought to him. Since he was not able to pay, the master ordered that he and his wife and his children, and all that he had, be sold to repay the debt. The servant fell on his knees before him. *'Be patient with me,'* he begged, *'and I will pay back everything.'* The servant's master took pity on him, canceled the debt and let him go.

"But when that servant went out, he found one of his fellow servants who owed him a hundred denarii. He grabbed him and began to choke him. *'Pay back what you owe me!'* he demanded. His fellow servant fell to his knees and begged him, *'Be patient with me, and I will pay you back.'* But he refused. Instead, he went off and had the man thrown into prison until he could pay the debt. When the other servants saw what had happened, they were greatly distressed and went and told their master everything that had happened.

"Then the master called the servant in. *'You wicked servant,'* he said, *'I canceled all that debt of yours because you begged me to. Shouldn't you have had mercy on your fellow servant just as I had on you?'* In anger his master turned him over to the jailers to be tortured, until he should pay back all he owed." [Jesus then said] *'This is how my heavenly Father will treat each of you unless you forgive your brother from your heart.'"* Matthew 18:21-35

Secondly, there is another way to know if one is sincerely forgiving someone or not. Jesus said, *"Love your enemies and pray for those who persecute you."* When one has the ability to pray for those who have been acting unkindly, that caring behavior speaks volumes about the merciful goodness going on within. Yes, you may still feel hurt by the wrongdoing, but that is not the judge of the fact that you are being compassionate by praying for your "enemy".

Along with the theme of mercy, the absolute main subject matter of this book obviously has been proof of the afterlife, which I have laid down in a somewhat methodical and coherent way so that you may also come to believe and trust in God's promise of eternal life. And with that said, there will always be some people, with sharp tongues and thinking, who will try to explain away any clear proof of life after death. That's normal! We've all known a naysayer, they exist. For instance, if you see *"black"* they will see *"white."* Usually when people are this adamant about denying obvious evidence, they have a hidden agenda. I suspect one possible hidden agenda of an afterlife naysayer is *"to dodge accountability and responsibility."* If a cynic ever admitted that there is proof of the hereafter, they would therefore also have to believe in God. Many do not want to do that. Why? One reason being is that it would also be to admit we are no longer an end unto ourselves. In acknowledging the hereafter, one accepts the reality there is Someone we must ultimately be accountable to and who expects us to live our lives with a sense of duty and responsibility, kindness, compassion and humility. Many teens and adults do not want to do this.

Frequently, another question comes up, *"What is our age in the afterlife?"* That depends.   Similar to my Aunt Sarah and Cousin Kim, it appears as though when a person is welcomed into heaven because of having acquired purity of heart in this life or having been purged in the afterlife, the person immediately becomes regenerated to a youthful twenty – thirty-something. Essentially, the two non corporal components of our "trinity," the soul and spirit, they immediately take on the image of one's young-looking resurrected body, although it has not been yet received. The regenerated soul and spirit will eventually be reunited to a very youthful body on the day of the resurrection of the dead.

However, apparently individuals that go to Purgatory retain the age and condition that the soul and spirit was in at the time of death. That is why in the story of the homeless man who appeared to me, he was still wearing a tattered t-shirt, looked worn and his teeth were in bad condition. The more a person descends to lower levels of Purgatory (depending on the amount of suffering and purgation that is applied to cleanse the soul of selfishness, a hard heart and self-centeredness), the original age at the time of death is retained as well as a charring and blackening of their image, denoting great suffering, as it was in my father's life.

Lastly, in this same regard, some souls, for whatever reasons, are permitted by God to wander for a time after death, as it was in the case of Ida. That is why we always pray for eternal rest for our departed loved ones. It is also, most probably the reason we frequently see the cliché, R.I.P. (Rest in Peace) on gravestones. The souls that wander tend to take on the appearance of their dead body, pale and emaciated. Possibly, this wandering may be a state of "limbo" that is spoken of in Catholic spirituality.

Sadly, some souls drop off the "radar" at the time of death. These are individuals who never cultivated a Faith in God while they were alive and they were self-seeking, unkind, unrepentant and unmerciful to others. Persons in this situation retain their age at death; they do not have regeneration and immediately experience the eternal pains of hell in soul and spirit. At the time of the Resurrection, those individuals in hell will also be reunited with their bodies and together with their soul and spirit will experience the pains and sufferings of hell for an eternity.

It is safe to say that it's highly unlikely that these souls could ever appear here on earth or have discussion with us. It would be more realistic that the devil could counterfeit such an appearance in order to deceive. He has been known to appear even as the crucified Christ and the Blessed Mother for reasons of deception. So, we should never put anything past him. The way we know such afterlife appearances are authentic is the fact they always lead one to greater peace, forgiveness, charity and love. If these qualities do not grow and flourish after such an encounter, guess what? Someone has just been duped by the devil himself! Also, one's mind can play tricks too, but even these types of perceived encounters can never replicate the charity and peace of God when afterlife appearances are authentic.

Putting it all into perspective, because of the immeasurable mercy of God, most people go to Purgatory, or they wander until they figure things out (as in the case of Ida) or they go directly to heaven. One has to work very hard in this life at power, control, evil, hatred and self-centeredness in order to actually wind up in hell for an eternity. As it was in my brother's case, despite a self-centered "party lifestyle", his belief in God, the just consideration by God of his childhood abuse, my and my mother's prayers for him, along with his one genuine act of mercy, won him a wonderful place in Purgatory and a clear shot at going to heaven by God's mercy.

It is important to acknowledge that the real sins that get one into hell, and we should be most fearful of, are the diabolical sins of power, control, pride, arrogance and hatred. The sins connected with our animal nature such as lust and addiction, although bad, they do not necessarily determine eternal perdition. C. S. Lewis, in his bestselling book, *Mere Christianity* agrees. He once wrote, "Finally, though I have had to speak at some length about sex, I want to make it as clear as I possibly can that the center of Christian morality is not here. If anyone thinks that Christians regard unchastity as the supreme vice, he is quite wrong. The sins of the flesh are bad, but they are the least bad of all sins. All the worst pleasures are purely spiritual:

the pleasure of putting other people in the wrong, of bossing and patronizing and spoiling sport, and back-biting; the pleasures of power, of hatred. For there are two things inside me, competing with the human self which I must try to become. They are the Animal self, and the Diabolical self. The Diabolical self is the worse of the two. That is why a cold, self-righteous prig who goes regularly to church may be far nearer to hell than a prostitute. But, of course, it is better to be neither." (*Mere Christianity*, Chapter 15)

And now a word of caution; with all this discussion about the hereafter, please be aware that the counterfeit practice of "spiritism" is never a good idea. For example, calling up the spirits of the departed, Ouija-boards and incantations should never be practiced or participated in. We are not supposed to summon up souls from the other side. Their visitation strictly comes as a gift from God for the purpose of furthering charity, love, forgiveness and for the cultivation of peace and inspiration. People who practice spiritism, such as moving tables, ghost hunting and calling up souls, are collaborating with the devil himself. Those who do this sort of thing, such as diviners, seers and witches, are in danger of eternally harming themselves and those who go to them for advice. Whoever appears should always come as a gift from God and we should never pray for and request, or seek, after this gift.

It is also important to make perfectly clear that this book is neither about being a Conservative nor about being a Liberal. One should be neither! But everyone should be Merciful, with a capital "M!" For instance, when a Conservative is unkind, spiteful, insulting, hateful and judgmental toward a Liberal, God is no longer on the side of the Conservative. God is always on the side of the downtrodden, the despised and the rejected and in this case, the Liberal. Conversely, when a Liberal is aggressive, malicious, arrogant and judgmental toward a Conservative, God is no longer on the side of the Liberal. He supports the Conservative.

Why is this so? Jesus himself knew very well what it was like to be unjustly judged. The self-righteous priests of his day thought they could read the motives of the heart (*only* God can do that) and so they thought they had Jesus "all figured out." Jesus gets killed because of this horrible, judgmental, assuming behavior of the church leaders. Thus, whenever a person is being judged and maligned, God immediately is in solidarity with the persecuted one. That is why we should welcome persecution. It is the only way to know for certain that God is solidly on one's side. He empathizes with those who are being judged, because God first-hand knows what it is like to be treated in such an ill and assuming manner.

Along these same lines, the following post was recently published at our blog, www.HomelessInAmerica.BlogSpot.com

"When Jesus said, *'The poor you always have with you,'* (Mark 14:7), he was pointing out that we are sinful in permitting poverty. For his allusion is to, *'There will be no poor among you if only you will obey the voice of the Lord.'* (Deuteronomy 15:4-5)

"Therefore . . .

"There should be no liberals in America, just the merciful.

No conservatives, just the compassionate.

No liberals, just the forgiving.

No conservatives, just kindness.

No liberals, just the patient.

No conservatives, just love."

(*Liberals and Conservatives*

www.HomelessInAmerica.BlogSpot.com,

Sunday, June 6, 2010)

It is for this reason that we are never to criticize or condemn others. Jesus said, *"Do not judge others, and you will not be judged. For you will be treated as you treat others. The standard you use in judging is the standard by which you will be judged. And why worry about a speck in your friend's eye when you have a log in your own? How can you think of saying to your friend, 'Let me help you get rid of that speck in your eye,' when you can't see past the log in your own eye? Hypocrite! First get rid of the log in your own eye; then you will see well enough to deal with the speck in your friend's eye."* Matthew 7:1-5

On Monday, January 7, 2008, I was engaged in a vision, one that has implications about generously and lovingly extending out the proclamation of the Gospel just as Peter's vision had asked him to do in book of Acts, Chapter 10. If you are not familiar with his revelation, which allowed the "Good News" to be spread to non Jews, (most of us today benefiting from Peter's vision), here is the text, just as it appears in Acts:

"About noon the following day as they were on their journey and approaching the city, Peter went up on the roof to pray. He became hungry and wanted something to eat, and while the meal was being prepared, he fell into a trance. He saw heaven opened and something like a large sheet being let down to earth by its four corners. It contained all kinds of four-footed animals, as well as reptiles of the earth and birds of the air. Then a voice told him, *'Get up, Peter. Kill and eat.' 'Surely not, Lord!'* Peter replied. *'I have never eaten anything impure or unclean.'* The voice spoke to him a second time, *'Do not call anything impure that God has made clean.'* This happened three times, and immediately the sheet was taken back to heaven." Acts 10:9-16

And so it was. Peter wakes up, comes downstairs and immediately there is a knock at the door. Three men meet Peter and lead him a day's journey to Caesarea, to a man by the name of Cornelius, and by God's inspiration; Peter, open-mindedly, gave this Italian a shot at heaven too. Prior to this, they all thought heaven was only for the Jews. Some people today think heaven is only for those individuals that live in nice houses, have the "white picket fence" lifestyle and are deemed morally "religious" by society. It's a similar confusion the early church had about who goes to heaven, until God corrected the mistake with visions and inspirations from the Holy Spirit. The next vision uprights a modern misunderstanding of who gets invited to paradise.

In the early morning hours of one winter's day in January of 2008, I saw throngs of people all gathered together in one huge ballroom. Shockingly, not one person attending a great "ungala" was even close to "normal" by society's standards. I was touched by their endurance of overwhelming rejection, pain and anguish. Many were grossly overweight, uneducated, retarded, gay, marginalized, physically unattractive, migrants, immigrants and oppressed. As I looked around the room at each one and witnessed their anguish, I thought to myself, *"These poor people, they suffer so from the rejection, judging, and the persecution that they receive from others."* Pitifully, they looked up desperately calling out, *"Please help us!"* Next, what they said is truly significant. *"We are abused. Could you please speak up for us by proclaiming Christ's command, 'This is my commandment that you love one another as I have loved you.'"* [John 15:12]

Evidently, these poor souls have a message; calling out for mercy from the Church today – both Catholic and Protestant. Are we listening?

Ultimately, the poor, the broken, the persecuted and the marginalized have already suffered much more than the powerful and wealthy in this life, who usually can buy comfort, and more-often-than-not, they do. It is unlikely that the discomforted here will have to do much more suffering in Purgatory in the afterlife. However, the middle-class, rich and powerful who may never have experienced this sort of rejection and despisement, and who may never have hit rock bottom as the poor and some with addictions do, they will have to do something now to "bring the bottom up."

What is meant by that? Well, there are a variety of ways to "bring the bottom up." For instance, a comfortable wealthy or middle-class person could volunteer a few hours a week at a Rescue Mission. Another possible way would be to "live without" certain comforts. Recently, I read about an Atlanta family of four, that convinced each other to sell their $1.5 million home, give half to the poor and give half of their belongings as well. They chronicle their journey in a new book, *The Power of Half*, by Kevin and Hannah Selwan. Thus, by cultivating a Faith in God and finding ways to "bring the bottom up," by those who have never received the gift of "hitting rock bottom," is how the wealthy and powerful can make it directly into heaven.

Conclusion

And so, in closing, James, the brother of the Lord was right after all, *"Faith without works is dead!"* (James 2:26) Appropriately, now a James or "Jim" will have the last word in this book:

"Listen, my dear brothers: Has not God chosen those who are poor in the eyes of the world to be rich in faith and to inherit the kingdom he promised those who love him? But you have insulted the poor. Is it not the rich who are exploiting you? Are they not the ones who are dragging you into court? Are they not the ones who are slandering the noble name of him to whom you belong?

"If you really keep the royal law found in Scripture, *'Love your neighbor as yourself,'* you are doing right. But if you show favoritism, you sin and are convicted by the law as lawbreakers. For whoever keeps the whole law, and yet stumbles at just one point, is guilty of breaking all of it. For he who said, *'Do not commit adultery,'* also said, *'Do not murder.'* If you do not commit adultery but do commit murder, you have become a lawbreaker.

"Speak and act as those who are going to be judged by the law that gives freedom, because judgment without mercy will be shown to anyone who has not been merciful. Mercy triumphs over judgment!

"What good is it, my brothers, if a man claims to have faith but has no deeds? Can such faith save him? Suppose a brother or sister is without clothes and daily food. If one of you says to him, *'Go, I wish you well; keep warm and well fed,'* but does nothing about his physical needs, what good is it? In the same way, faith by itself, if it is not accompanied by action, is dead.

"But someone will say, *'You have faith; I have deeds.'* Show me your faith without deeds, and I will show you my faith by what I do. You believe that there is one God. Good! Even the demons believe that—and shudder." (James 12:5-19)

POSTLOGUE

An Invitation

Millions of homeless Americans are waiting for someone just like you to extend to them mercy and the conversation of this book. The *Servants of the Father of Mercy* is an Ecumenical Christian family and welcomes people of Faith to join our team as lay volunteer "Missioners," helping just five hours a month to serve homeless men, women and children in your very own community. Won't you contact us today and consider "bringing the bottom up" by joining our community? For more information, email <u>Contact@ServantsoftheFather.org</u>.

Also, our religious vocations for Catholic Brothers, Sisters, Priests and Deacons are open to those individuals of all ages, eighteen and older, who are in touch with their own brokenness and poverty. We look for former fishermen, prostitutes, the uneducated, despised and rejected to come and share our mission. Get the discussion going by emailing us at: Vocations@ServantsoftheFather.org.

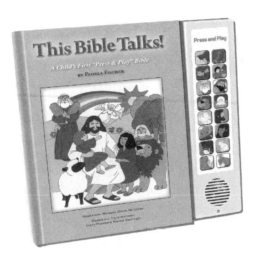

Annually at Christmastime, the *Servants of the Father of Mercy* look to donate our children's "Press & Play" talking Bible, *This Bible Talks!* to poor and homeless children living in America and on the global mission field. We believe there is a great need, in these growing tumultuous times, to urgently form toddlers and pre-readers early on in their developmental years with the Word of God. You can discover more about the mission and how to support it at www.ServantsoftheFather.org and www.ThisBibleTalks.com.

Please continue the conversation of this book and subscribe to www.HomelessinAmerica.BlogSpot.com, America's only journal for triumphal insights into everyone's poverty, illusions and brokenness. Ask your family and friends to subscribe too!

You are invited to donate alms of mercy and compassion to the homeless, providing them with snacks, fresh fruits and vegetables, beverages, clothing and spiritual supplies. Even the smallest donation can provide bottles of water – preventing dehydration and even the untimely death of a homeless person. Give online at www.ServantsoftheFather.org or by posting checks to: *Servants of the Father of Mercy, Inc.,* P.O. Box 42001, Los Angeles, CA 90042.

Servants of the Father of Mercy, Inc. is a Private Association within the Archdiocese of Los Angeles and it's listed in the O.C.D. (Official Catholic Directory). It is a non-profit, tax-exempt 501 (c) (3) organization. All donations are tax deductible. Visit us on the web at www.ServantsoftheFather.org.

ADDENDUM

Help the Homeless in Purgatory

Some estimates approximate billions of souls could still remain homeless in Purgatory at this present time, and for the moment, they are unable to access their eternal home. St. John Vianey once said, *"Yet how quickly we could empty Purgatory if we but really wished to."* Possibly he is referring to a special prayer that can bring these poor souls home, as told to St. Gertrude the Great (+ November 17, 1301) by the Lord himself. He indicated the following prayer would release 1,000 souls from Purgatory each time it is said:

> Eternal Father, I offer You the Most Precious
> Blood of Your Divine Son, Jesus, in union with
> the Masses said throughout the world today,
> for all the Holy Souls in Purgatory, for sinners
> everywhere, for sinners in the Universal Church,
> those in my own home and within my family. Amen.

Upon one's own death, why risk the possibility of personal poverty and hardships in purgatory? The next set of prayers listed below prevent afterlife "homelessness" and honor the seven times Jesus spilled His Precious Blood for us, as revealed by Our Lady to St. Bridget and approved by the popes Clement XII and Innocent X.

7 PRAYERS OF ST. BRIDGET
SAID DAILY FOR 12 YEARS

Our Lord Made 5 Promises To Saint Bridget

If the soul praying these seven prayers dies before the entire twelve years have been completed, the Lord will accept them as having been prayed in their entirety, because the intention of the soul was to complete them as directed. If a day or a few days are missed due to a valid reason, they can be made up for later, at the soul's earliest opportunity. Our Lord made these five Promises to anyone who recited/prayed these prayers daily for twelve entire years:

1. The soul who prays them will suffer no Purgatory.
2. The soul who prays them will be accepted among the Martyrs as though he had spilled his blood for his faith.
3. The soul who prays them can choose three others whom Jesus will then keep in a state of grace sufficient to become holy.
4. No one in the four successive generations of the soul who prays them will be lost.
5. The soul who prays them will be made conscious of his death one month in advance.

The 7 Prayers of Saint Bridget

Opening Prayer - O Jesus, now I wish to pray the Lord's Prayer seven times in unity with the love with which You sanctified this prayer in Your Heart. Take it from my lips into Your Divine Heart. Improve and complete it so much that it brings as much honor and joy to the Trinity as You granted it on earth with this prayer. May these pour upon Your Holy Humanity in Glorification to Your Painful Wounds and the Precious Blood that You spilled from them.

1st Prayer - The Circumcision: Pray 1 Our Father: Our Father who art in heaven, hallowed be thy name; thy kingdom come; thy will be done on earth as it is in heaven. Give us this day our daily bread; and forgive us our trespasses as we forgive those who trespass against us; and lead us not into temptation, but deliver us from evil. Amen

Pray 1 Hail Mary: Hail Mary full of grace. The Lord is with thee. Blessed art thou among women, and blessed is the fruit of thy womb, Jesus. Holy Mary, Mother of God, pray for us sinners, now and at the hour of our death. Amen.

Eternal Father, through Mary's unblemished hands and the Divine Heart of Jesus, I offer You the first wounds, the first pains, and the first Bloodshed as atonement for my and all of humanity's sins of youth, as protection against the first mortal sin, especially among my relatives.

2nd Prayer - The Suffering on the Mount of Olives: Pray 1 Our Father, 1 Hail Mary

Eternal Father, through Mary's unblemished hands and the Divine Heart of Jesus, I offer You the terrifying suffering of Jesus' Heart on the Mount of Olives and every drop of His Bloody Sweat as atonement for my and all of humanity's sins of the heart, as protection against such sins and for the spreading of Divine and brotherly Love.

3rd Prayer - The Flogging: Pray 1 Our Father, 1 Hail Mary

Eternal Father, through Mary's unblemished hands and the Divine Heart of Jesus, I offer You the many thousands of Wounds, the gruesome Pains, and the Precious Blood of the Flogging as atonement for my and all of humanity's sins of the Flesh, as protection against such sins and the preservation of innocence, especially among my relatives.

4th Prayer - The Crowning of Thorns: Pray 1 Our Father, 1 Hail Mary

Eternal Father, through Mary's unblemished hands and the Divine Heart of Jesus, I offer You the Wounds, the Pains, and the Precious Blood of Jesus' Holy Head from the Crowning with Thorns as atonement for my and all of humanity's sins of the Spirit, as protection against such sins and the spreading of Christ's kingdom here on earth.

5th Prayer - The Carrying of the Cross: Pray 1 Our Father, 1 Hail Mary

Eternal Father, through Mary's unblemished hands and the Divine Heart of Jesus, I offer You the Sufferings on the way of the Cross, especially His Holy Wound on His Shoulder and its Precious Blood as atonement for my and all of humanity's rebellion against the Cross, every grumbling against Your Holy Arrangements and all other sins of the tongue, as protection against such sins and for true love of the Cross.

6th Prayer - The Crucifixion: Pray 1 Our Father, 1 Hail Mary

Eternal Father, through Mary's unblemished hands and the Divine Heart of Jesus, I offer You Your Son on the Cross, His Nailing and Raising, His Wounds on the Hands and Feet and the three streams of His Precious Blood that poured forth from these for us, His extreme tortures of the Body and Soul, His precious Death and its non-bleeding Renewal in all Holy Masses on earth as atonement for all wounds against vows and regulations within the Orders, as reparation for my and all of the world's sins, for the sick and the dying, for all holy priests and laymen, for the Holy Father's intentions toward the restoration of Christian families, for the strengthening of Faith, for our country and unity among all nations in Christ and His Church, as well as for the Diaspora.

7th Prayer - The Piercing of Jesus' Side: Pray 1 Our Father, 1 Hail Mary

Eternal Father, accept as worthy, for the needs of the Holy Church and as atonement for the sins of all Mankind, the Precious Blood and Water which poured forth from the Wound of Jesus' Divine Heart. Be gracious and merciful toward us. Blood of Christ, the last precious content of His Holy Heart, wash me of all my and others' guilt of sin! Water from the Side of Christ, wash me clean of all punishments for sin and extinguish the flames of Purgatory for me and for all the Poor Souls. Amen.

Durable, laminated copies are available of Saint Bridget's 7 Prayers, by donation. Each is 8.5 x 11 and perfect to take along in a brief case or backpack, as well as laying it on a night stand or coffee table, wearing well for twelve years with normal daily use. Specify English or Spanish. For more information, email Info@ServantsoftheFather.org, or write: SFM, P.O. Box 42001, Los Angeles, CA 90042

Recommended Reading

C. S. Lewis, <u>Mere Christianity</u>, New York, MacMillan Publishing Company, 1978.

Henri Nouwen, <u>The Return of the Prodigal Son</u>, New York, Doubleday, 1994.

Jean Vanier, <u>A Door of Hope</u>, London, Hodder & Stoughton, 1999.

John of the Cross, <u>Selected Writings - Classics of Western Spirituality</u>, trans. Kieran Kavanaugh, New York, Paulist Press, 1987.

Mike Yankoski, <u>Under the Overpass</u>, Colorado Springs, Multnomah Books, 2005.

Nicky Eltz, <u>Get Us Out of Here - Maria Simma Speaks with Nicky Eltz</u>, Dekalb, Illinois, The Medjugorje Web, 2005.

Saint Augustine, <u>City of God</u>, trans. Marcus D. D. Dods, New York, Modern Library, 1950.

Saint Augustine, <u>Confessions</u>, trans. Henry Chadwick, New York, Oxford University Press, 2009.

Saint Maria Faustina Kowalska, <u>Divine Mercy in My Soul - The Diary of Sister Faustina Kowalska</u>, Stockbridge, MA, Marian Press, 1987.

Simon Tugwell, <u>The Beatitudes: Soundings in Christian Tradition</u>, Darton, Longman & Todd Ltd., Great Britain, Templegate Publishers, 1980.

<u>The Little Flowers of St. Francis</u>, trans. Raphael Brown, Garden City, NY: Hanover House, 1958.

Teresa of Avila, <u>The Collected Works of Teresa of Avila</u>, 3 vol., trans. Kieran Kavanaugh, Washington, D.C., ICS Publications, 2001.

How to Order this Book for Your Church, Prayer Group, Family and Friends

On the Internet, you may conveniently order additional copies of *Proof of the Afterlife – The Conversation Continues*, at www.ServantsoftheFather.org.

Quantity discounts are available for churches, prayer groups and hospitals, as well as discussion and support groups. Send your email request to Info@ServantsoftheFather.org, with the number of books, your name, phone number and "ship to" address information, or post the same in a letter to:

PROOF OF THE AFTERLIFE
Servants of the Father of Mercy
P. O. Box 42001, Los Angeles, CA 90042

Get in touch with the author to schedule a group presentation or speaking engagement by sending an email request to Contact@ServantsoftheFather.org.